Soaring
Living Empowered and Joyful

MATTI DOBBS, PH.D.

BALBOA.
PRESS

A DIVISION OF HAY HOUSE

Editors: Marlene Oulton, www.MarleneOulton.com and
Gwen Hoffnagle, www.GwenHoffnagle.com

Balboa Press books may be ordered through booksellers or by contacting:

Balboa Press
A Division of Hay House
1663 Liberty Drive
Bloomington, IN 47403
www.balboapress.com
1 (877) 407-4847

Because of the dynamic nature of the Internet, any web addresses or
links contained in this book may have changed since publication and may
no longer be valid. The views expressed in this work are solely those
of the author and do not necessarily reflect the views of the publisher,
and the publisher hereby disclaims any responsibility for them.

The author of this book does not dispense medical advice or prescribe the use
of any technique as a form of treatment for physical, emotional, or medical
problems without the advice of a physician, either directly or indirectly. The
intent of the author is only to offer information of a general nature to help
you in your quest for emotional and spiritual well-being. In the event you use
any of the information in this book for yourself, which is your constitutional
right, the author and the publisher assume no responsibility for your actions.

Any people depicted in stock imagery provided by Thinkstock are models,
and such images are being used for illustrative purposes only.
Certain stock imagery © Thinkstock.

Print information available on the last page.

ISBN: 978-1-5043-2814-2 (sc)
ISBN: 978-1-5043-2815-9 (e)

Library of Congress Control Number: 2015902591

Balboa Press rev. date: 04/30/2015

CONTENTS

ACKNOWLEDGMENTS

This book is dedicated to my mother, Mattie Louise Fountain, who first empowered me to *soar* through her love, and to my husband, Dr. Harold E. Mavritte, who not only loves and *soars* with me, he creates the space for me to *soar*.

I am grateful to my family, my sister Iola, and to the nieces who insisted that I write this book to share with others the wisdom I have lovingly shared with them. I want to thank my friend, the late Dr. Jane Claypool, who recognized the power in *Soaring*, for her support and encouragement over the years, particularly in writing this book.

I also thank my dear friend and colleague, Spiritual Director Debby O'Donnell, for her love and support and for creating an environment for me and others to *soar*. I also appreciate the support of my friends at the Center for Spiritual Living in Carlsbad, California, whose very presence in my life inspires me to *soar*.

I am deeply grateful to all the people who invited me into their lives and shared their journeys with me, and in the process taught me to *soar*. I am particularly appreciative of the people who generously agreed to share their stories in this book to help others *soar*.

Finally, I extend deep gratitude to my editors, Marlene Oulton and Gwen Hoffnagle, for their patience and professionalism in editing this book.

INTRODUCTION

Soaring is a spiritual journey. *Soaring* shows you how to turn the invisible into the visible, how to turn your hopes and dreams into reality. This book taps in to the deepest recesses of your soul and your innermost thoughts to clarify what you want from your life. It is a guide to knowing yourself more intimately and connecting with your spiritual center to live life more fully, empowered, and joy-filled. *Soaring* is living your best life. You know who you are and where you are going, and you use Divine guidance and your own inner resources to get you there.

My career has been devoted to helping people live their best life. In various roles such as social worker, mental health therapist, organizational consultant, life coach, and spiritual leader, my aim has been to inspire individuals to new levels of thinking and being – to change their world-view. These *Flight Lessons,* as I call them, reflect changes in my spiritual consciousness to levels of knowing and being that transcend everyday living. I *soar.* The aim of this book is to share with you some of the lessons I learned along the way.

Soaring is about my journey, my story, and the stories of others I've met in my quest to inspire others to achieve their dreams. The stories in this book are real.

Some are composites of more than one story. The names and identifying information have been changed to protect each individual's identity.

This book grew out of a request from a group of women who attended my workshops over the years to design a session exclusively for them. They wanted special attention to where they were in life at that time, which was a much different place from where they had been in the skill-building workshops they had attended in the past. Most had successfully climbed the corporate ladder, pursued their "what's next" goals, and were feeling a sense of ennui. Basically they were asking themselves, "Where do we go from here?"

So we spent the weekend looking at our lives, exploring our successes, where we had been, the low points and the high points, where we were, and what was next. We put together action plans and followed up with added sessions to see if we were exploring the next steps in our lives, namely *living joyfully and empowered* as we pursued our next adventures.

Soaring grew out of that weekend and my own aspiration to live each day happy, inspired, and in love with life. These women had arrived at points in their lives where they were learning that life is not all about the "doing" – it is not all about achieving or amassing the outward signs of success, nor is it about your "stuff." It is living in love and joy, and nurturing your spirit. It is "being" perfect, whole, and complete in your mind as you consciously plan and take the next steps on your own wonderful journey.

You may be a student, a young or mid-career professional, or someone who simply wants to enjoy a spirit-centered life of meaning and purpose. *Soaring* was written for individuals who want more: more joy, more love, more peace, more meaning in their lives. *Soaring provides a roadmap for individuals who desire to live their lives fully engaged, inspired, and in charge!*

I invite you to take this spiritual journey with me.

FLIGHT LESSON ONE

The *Soaring* Flight Plan

Come with me for a stroll on the beach. As we walk together, visualize the waves ebbing and flowing and crashing against the shore. See the birds ascending and descending as they flit about on this beautiful sunlit day. And as you watch the birds, pay attention to the different levels of energy they require in their flight. Notice the difference in the amount of energy they expend taking off and landing versus that which is required once they reach *soaring* altitude. When the birds reach their desired height, they level off, relax their wings, and effortlessly propel themselves through the air by gently flapping their wings. They simply let go and allow Spirit to take over. I call this seemingly effortless flying *soaring.* The aim of this book is to help you *soar...* to help you achieve new levels of awareness and joy in your life. It's about recognizing and using your spiritual power.

Soaring is a state of being – an intrinsic happiness and joy you have when living a life of purpose. It is living your best life from the deep recesses of your soul. It is living life in sweet communion and connection with your higher self. It is living a spiritual life. *Soaring* is a journey that takes you inward to who you are and what you want your life to be. It is living life joyously, empowered, and in charge.

Many have questioned how to take the next steps in their lives. Here are a couple of stories from people who have gone on similar journeys:

> Vera decided to attend Olympic track-and-field training camp in San Diego rather than pursue graduate school or a career. Our first discussion revealed that although Vera was on a trajectory to *soar*, she was feeling uncertain and alone in a new environment even though she was pursuing her dream. She questioned what to do next and how to handle her next quest fully empowered and in charge. Through coaching she designed *an action plan and charted the steps to help her feel more in control of her life.* As a result, she is currently at the Olympic Training Center, has a part-time position, and is feeling more acclimated to life in Southern California as she trains for the gold.

> Allen is a forty-year-old physical therapist who had reached a point in his career where he wanted change. He performed research at a local university to stimulate and inspire him. He was feeling restless and wondered, "What's next for me to do in my life, especially in my career?" To his amazement, his friends shared this

same feeling. At that point in their lives in a downward economy, they felt it was a lot harder to change jobs, careers, or lifestyles. Yet their underlying feelings were, "What's next? How do I move on from here?" Allen's visioning uncovered his real passion to be a researcher. He examined his options and over time located a full-time position in this field.

What was next for both these individuals was bringing more joy and meaning into their lives. No matter where we find ourselves as we develop a plan to get from A to B, it is important to ask ourselves, "What is my passion? What gives me joy? What is it that I want to do with my life right now? Better yet, am I doing it?"

Soaring involves envisioning your hopes, dreams, and aspirations, and charting action plans to achieve them. It is a metaphysical process in which you recognize that you live in a spiritual Universe in which your thoughts create your world, and you consciously learn to tap in to your inner resources and Divine connection to achieve the life you desire. You are reading this book because something within you wants to change. You want to express life more fully. The question is how do you get there from here?

Soaring is living in spiritual awareness, knowing that we are supported by a loving and abundant Universe. It is developing a consciousness in which we realize that we co-create our worlds and live in a state of joy and fulfillment at all times because everything around us is flowing in Divine order, no matter what the circumstances or facts of our present existence might be.

Soaring is recognizing our connection to the Divine. It is living in the awareness that there is a Universal Energy throughout the Universe and that we are one with this Energy. Some call it God. Some call it Spirit. Some call it Buddha. Whatever name we attach to this Higher Power, each of us co-creates our world using this Invisible Force.

Whether you accomplish this consciously or unconsciously, it is the way of life. The difference between the successful and unsuccessful person is that the successful person consciously uses their own creative power. You have only to recognize it and use it.

Recognizing your oneness with the Source of all life that I call Spirit empowers you to *soar.* You can access this spiritual power for it is a part of you. It is your connection to Source. Call it Divine guidance. It is that inner wisdom, your higher self, that speaks to you when you are quiet and listen. The important thing is to know that Spirit is within each of us. Through this power within you co-create your world. This is the foundation for *soaring.* It is living consciously, embodying the belief that there is a Universal Power, a Creative Intelligence in all, through all, and that each of us can access this power and use it to co-create a world of joy and happiness of our choosing.

People who *soar* consciously use their innate creative power to co-create their worlds. You feel a sense of your own power! You believe in yourself! Nothing can stop you from achieving your purpose. You dream, set energy in motion, and enjoy the ride complete with life's ups and downs. You might be thinking, "Where do

I begin? How do I commence this exciting flight? What do I have to do?"

The *Soaring* Flight Plan

The **Soaring Flight Plan**, a step-by-step approach to living a *soaring* lifestyle, is described in Figure 1 in this chapter. It consists of twelve *Flight Lessons* of transformational tools and levels of awareness to help you *soar*. It is built on a spiritual foundation, a belief in a Higher Power, God, or Spirit – whatever you choose to call it. In the rest of the book I call it Spirit and Higher Power, among other names. Each time I use these names I am referring to whatever Higher Power you wish to envision.

Flight Lesson One describes the **Soaring Flight Plan** and what it means to *soar*. *Flight Lesson Two, Awakening Your Spirituality*, provides the mental preparation or attitude to *soar*. In *Flight Lesson Three, Developing Your Flight Plan*, you clarify your purpose, identify your personal goals, and create an action plan to achieve them. *Flight Lesson Four* teaches you to *Visualize It! Picture It! Affirm It!* to achieve your goals. *Flight Lesson Five* encourages *Igniting Love* in your life as a way to a happier lifestyle.

Flight Lesson Six discusses the benefits and impact of gratitude and ways to make it a part of your life as it encourages *Lifting Off with Gratitude*. *Flight Lesson Seven, Praying to Increase Altitude,* discusses ways to connect with Spirit as a source of joy and meaning.

Flight Lesson Eight explores *Meditating to Regenerate Your Spirit. Flight Lesson Nine, Forgiving to Forget,* focuses on forgiveness as a means to let go of negative energy and move forward in life. *Encountering Turbulence, Flight Lesson Ten,* provides tools to surrender; to let go and overcome life obstacles using spiritual resolve and faith. *Flight Lesson Eleven, Nurturing Mind, Body, and Spirit,* shares information to support your whole body physically, mentally, emotionally, and spiritually. *Flight Lesson Twelve, SOARING: Living Empowered and Joyful,* integrates all the *Flight Lessons* and explores what *soaring* feels like.

Mastering the life-enhancing practices in these *Flight Lessons* supports you as you move from low-vibration behaviors such as worry and doubt to a *soaring* attitude of confidence, *knowing* that you are empowered and supported by your Higher Power. Whatever you want and need is available to you. You let go of mediocrity and embrace a new level of awareness and being. You move to *soaring* altitude. You see life from a new perspective. To learn these transformational skills and incorporate them into your life requires practice – spiritual practice. Each chapter includes practice sessions to integrate the *Flight Lessons* into your life.

Progress in the **Soaring Flight Plan** does not necessarily occur sequentially. Take the **Soaring Self-Assessment** at the end of this chapter to determine in what areas you desire to focus your attention. You may rate your overall satisfaction with life as high, yet find you have specific work to do in another area such as nurturing your mind, body, and spirit.

The *Soaring* Flight Plan

Flight Lesson Twelve
Soaring: Living Empowered and Joyful

⬆

Flight Lesson Eleven
Nurturing Mind, Body, and Spirit

⬆

Flight Lesson Ten
Encountering Turbulence

⬆

Flight Lesson Nine
Forgiving to Forget

⬆

Flight Lesson Eight
Meditating to Regenerate Your Spirit

⬆

Flight Lesson Seven
Praying to Increase Altitude

⬆

Flight Lessons

Flight Lesson Six
Lifting Off with Gratitude

⬆

Flight Lesson Five
Igniting Love

⬆

Flight Lesson Four
Visualize It! Picture It! Affirm It!

⬆

Flight Lesson Three
Developing Your Flight Plan

⬆

Flight Lesson Two
Awakening Your Spirituality

⬆

Flight Lesson One
The *Soaring* Flight Plan

Universal Energy

Figure 1

Jan's story below illustrates that phenomenal success in one area of your life may still leave other areas lacking, and the need for additional work and focus in that particular *Flight Lesson*.

> Jan, a fifty-four-year-old triathlete, rates the quality of her life as *soaring* on the **Soaring Self-Assessment**. In thirteen hours of competition consisting of swimming 2.4 miles, cycling 112 miles, and running 26.2 miles without a break, Jan shows resilience and determination. She is a former abuser of cocaine, methamphetamine, and cigarettes. Although Jan was attracted to athleticism at an early age, she did little with that inclination. She entered abusive relationships, was drawn to addiction again and again, consistently hitting low points in her life, until she met her current husband who helped her heal through love.
>
> Jan stumbled onto her life's purpose in a gym when her husband's cousin noticed her natural athletic ability and trained Jan to teach fitness classes. She credits love, determination, belief in her Higher Power, and the synchronicity of Spirit in placing opportunities before her as the reasons for her success.
>
> Jan demonstrates success in several areas of the **Soaring Flight Plan**. After moving the bar upward in several levels of physical competition, she now feels that she can do anything. She motivates others

through her job as a personal trainer, and even encourages weary racers to run in her energy and talks them through to the finish line.

Jan is generous and giving. To sustain her body while racing, she created healthy endurance treats that she cuts into mini bites to eat while running. After sharing them at the gym where she worked, she received a request to create the bites for a major distributor, taking the business from inception to national distribution in six months.

Although Jan is *soaring* overall, she arrived there unconsciously and is now consciously developing a new plan for her life. She still has healing to do in the area of self-love, and sobriety is an ongoing challenge. Jan has a vision of restarting her mini bites business, which is currently in hiatus. Having accomplished success in the athletic field, she now wants to repeat that success again in the business world and is developing a new personal flight plan in *Flight Lesson Three*.

My hope is that as you explore these transformational practices and incorporate them into your life you will transform your way of thinking and being. Your attitude will change. As your attitude changes, your altitude changes, and you *soar.* Let's get started.

Applying This *Flight Lesson* in Your Life

1. Complete the **Soaring Self-Assessment** (Figure 2) to ascertain your level of satisfaction with your life now in regard to the qualities considered important to a *soaring* lifestyle.

2. Any qualities marked with a six or less are considered *Flight Lessons* to focus on to enhance your life satisfaction. You may choose to pay particular attention to these lessons.

The *Soaring* Self-Assessment

Please complete the assessment below by circling the number that best describes your level of satisfaction with the quality of your life in the following areas with 1 being low and 10 being high satisfaction.

Low 1 2 3 4 5 6 7 8 9 10 High

Quality of Life	Level of Satisfaction	Score
1. I am spiritual	1 2 3 4 5 6 7 8 9 10	___
2. I am clear on my life purpose	1 2 3 4 5 6 7 8 9 10	___
3. I have a vision for my life	1 2 3 4 5 6 7 8 9 10	___
4. I love myself	1 2 3 4 5 6 7 8 9 10	___
5. I am grateful	1 2 3 4 5 6 7 8 9 10	___
6. I have satisfying relationships	1 2 3 4 5 6 7 8 9 10	___
7. I pray	1 2 3 4 5 6 7 8 9 10	___
8. I meditate	1 2 3 4 5 6 7 8 9 10	___
9. I have no unresolved forgiveness	1 2 3 4 5 6 7 8 9 10	___
10. I handle life challenges well	1 2 3 4 5 6 7 8 9 10	___
11. I practice self-care	1 2 3 4 5 6 7 8 9 10	___
12. I am health-conscious	1 2 3 4 5 6 7 8 9 10	___
13. My overall satisfaction with my life	1 2 3 4 5 6 7 8 9 10	___
	Total	___

Scoring
Each life quality is important to a *Soaring* lifestyle and your overall sense of happiness and well-being. To obtain your score, total the numbers you circled.

Scoring Key
100 – 130: You are *soaring*. Are there qualities that you would like to enhance? Enjoy your flight!

90 – 99: You are soaring at moderate altitude. Life can be so much more. Identify your areas of focus.

89 and below: Are you ready to increase your altitude? Buckle up. We are in for a ride!

Figure 2

FLIGHT LESSON TWO

Awakening Your Spirituality

In this *Flight Lesson* you'll awaken the power within you – your spirituality. We live in a Spiritual Universe in which we are all connected. We are intimately connected with the Divine as well as with everything and everyone else in the Universe. We are all one. The Universal Energy that created you is the same Energy that causes the Earth to rotate on its axis with precision. The same energy allows us to know what time it is in New York as well as in the Far East. It is also the Energy that pulls the waves rhythmically toward the shore with such accuracy that scientists can calculate their height and force and surfers can assess whether or not that day will be a good surfing day. It is Intelligence that tells the flowers when to bloom, the leaves to turn color, and the daffodils to poke out their heads after a frost.

This Intelligence is within you. Think about it; when was the last time you reminded yourself to breathe, your heart to beat, or your skin to heal a wound? Some call this Intelligence Divine Energy, Universal Energy, Love, Dharma, Buddha, Mind, or Spirit, among other names. The philosopher Ernest Holmes called it a Power for Good. Ralph Waldo Emerson called it the Over-Soul.

Dr. Wayne Dyer refers to it as Inspiration. Whatever you choose to call it, it's a deeper awareness of your spirituality and your connection to the whole of life, and tapping in to it is the foundation for *soaring* – living your life empowered and joyful.

The fuel for this flight is your knowledge that there is a Higher Power in the Universe, and you can access it through your mind. Spirit is Omnipotent, Omniscient, and Omnipresent. It is all-powerful, all-knowing, and everywhere present. Your mind is the navigational system on this flight. Tapping in to Divine wisdom through your mind empowers you to *soar.*

Life Is Calling

There are spiritual principles operating in the Universe. These laws, as they are also called, have been passed down through the ages, and explain the creative process in nature as well as in the individual. Knowledge of these laws empowers you to *soar.*

In the *Seven Spiritual Laws of Success*, Deepak Chopra describes the first law as the Law of Pure Potentiality. In our essential state each of us is pure consciousness, pure potentiality, and infinite possibility. That is our spiritual essence.

The Universe is calling you to higher expressions of life; higher expressions of what you came here to be. Who are you and what did you come here to do? Are you doing it? Are you happy with where you are right now? Are you getting what you want out of life? Are you where you want to be? Are there new mountains you have yet to climb?

We are all unique expressions of Spirit. Feelings of discontent, those questions like "Is there something else for me to be?" "Something else for me to do?" and "What's next?" are calls of the Universe to higher expressions of yourself. According to Eric Butterworth in *The Universe Is Calling*, "*It is a restless urge that keeps you forever reaching for the highest, and is incapable of settling for anything less.*"

Our spirituality is a call to connection. Eckhart Tolle, author of *A New Earth,* tells us that our purpose here is to awaken to our spirituality, and that this awakening leads to intrinsic joy and happiness.

> I was living the good life in Brentwood, California, with a successful career, happily married to a brilliant, Renaissance man. I lived in a house on a hill with views of the canyon, the city, and the ocean. My life was working really well fiscally and materially. I drove a high-powered sports car. Young and beautiful, the wind was at my back. Then one day I remembered this scripture: "*To whom much is given, much is required*" (Luke 12:48). I had been raised in the church so I was very familiar with this statement. Now, having fun living a wonderful life, I no longer devoted time to my spiritual life.
>
> Something within me knew there was *more!* Something within me said, "Life is more

than this. Seek it!" It was the call to come up a little higher in spiritual consciousness. It was a call to prayer and connection with Spirit.

When my first husband and I set our individual and joint goals at the beginning of that year, I set an intention to renew my spirituality. When I looked at my goals mid-year and realized I had made no progress, I joined the nearest church. Meanwhile, I walked the beach daily. One day on the way back to our home, I walked inland and wandered into a church bookstore and perused the literature that spoke to me. Something within me was yearning for connection.

Spirit knew what was ahead for me and that I had a high mountain to climb, so It was getting me ready for the task ahead. As sung in the old Scottish folk song and Irish blessing, *"The long time sun was guiding my way on."* My husband, whom I deeply loved, was going to transition to eternity, and I would need spiritual resolve to navigate the rough waters ahead. During that dark night of my soul, Spirit became my guiding force. To make a long story short, I was pushed, pulled, and guided by Spirit to let go of ego and find my true essence, my life in Spirit.

While most people move forward because they are seeking something wonderful, others discover that their response to a crisis can be great motivation. People speak of finding gifts, for example, in illness, the 9/11 aftermath, or the Boston Marathon bombing. They experience a proverbial wake-up call. Some people get tired of drifting along with the tide, going nowhere in particular, living life at a low vibration level with no real passion, or simply working hard and asking no questions from life.

Where are you in your unfolding? If you're feeling unfulfilled, where would you like to begin your journey? What if your life is working well and you want even greater experiences? If this sounds like you, set your intention to live at an even higher vibration in Spirit. Tell yourself, "Life can be better than this." Make a decision to live life out loud, empowered and with joy!

Developing a *Soaring* Consciousness

Your consciousness is your belief system – how you view the world. Is your world a loving, friendly place, or is it fearful and ego-driven? An important part of your **Soaring Flight Plan** is building a *soaring* consciousness or a *soaring* attitude toward life. Each *Flight Lesson* shares a *soaring* practice important to developing a *soaring* consciousness. The fundamental tenets of a *soaring* attitude toward life are:

- Believe in a Higher Power and yourself.

- Know that your thoughts have power; the Power is within you.

- Feel love, the basic energy of the Universe.

People who *soar* believe in themselves. They have an attitude of *Yes I can!* Most of all they believe in an Infinite Power in the Universe, a Source of wholeness and goodness that is available to them by right of Divine grace. The Master Teacher, Jesus, said, "The kingdom of God is within you" (Luke 17:21). Although there are many interpretations as to what this means, I interpret it to mean that the Power is within you. Given free will, you co-create your experiences through your own volition and personal choices in alignment with Spirit.

You Are Unlimited

You can do anything, have anything, and be anything you want to be through the power of your mind and belief in yourself. First create it in your mind. It is not just about the doing and the having. The real key is to do so in a spirit of love, peace, and joy, without fear, worry, or doubt, because you are certain that Spirit is supporting you.

> Oprah Winfrey was born in a small rural town in Mississippi. She overcame poverty and hardship and rose to acclaim as a talk show host through her focus on self-help and spiritual issues. A billionaire, she is one of the richest self-made women in America, yet continues to focus on philanthropy and ways to share her spirituality with the nation and the international community. Oprah attributes her success to her spiritual and educational foundation. *"All that I am or will ever become is because of my spiritual*

foundation and my educational foundation. My life is a living testimony to what God can do with a human being." (Associated Press, November 11, 2002, as reported in *The World According to Oprah* by Ken Lawrence.)

ॐ ॐ ॐ

Renowned motivational speaker and best-selling author Lisa Nichols rose from the welfare rolls to become an international multimillionaire. In her book *No Matter What*, Lisa confessed that although she was featured in the hit film and book *The Secret*, and traveled around the world speaking about the Law of Attraction, she was guided by a different law, the one she calls the "Law of No Matter What." No matter what the circumstances, she was determined to set her inner champion free and live the life of her dreams.

Both these women overcame extraordinary circumstances to achieve significant success, and you can, too.

You are supported and guided. You are connected to Spirit. How do you connect with Spirit? You may be asking, "If Spirit is all around me, why do I not see It in my life? More than that, what do I need to do to make It a part of me? How do I awaken my Divine potential, the Spirit within?" Another important principle in achieving your goals is that your mind is the creative cause of all that occurs in your life.

Our Thoughts Have Power

We create our worlds through our belief systems, one thought at a time. Begin with a belief in your own unlimited potential. "Me, unlimited?" you might ask. "What have I done that is significant? If I am unlimited, why am I not rich? Why are all these negative things showing up in my life?"

Our thoughts have power. What we think about, we bring about. *"Thoughts are things,"* said philosopher Ernest Holmes. Teachers through the ages have spoken about our ability to create what we want in our lives through the power of our minds. The expression "You reap what you sow" speaks to the power of our thoughts. When we plant a seed (a thought) in the fertile soil of our minds, we produce a result. Ernest Holmes called this the Law of Cause and Effect. Deepak Chopra refers to this law as Karma. Each action has a reaction, and so it is with our thoughts.

Thoughts are creative. Each manifestation (representation in form) first begins as an idea. The Wright brothers believed that vehicles could fly. Ben Franklin generated electricity from a key and a kite. Someone's vision to ride in wagons and automobiles led to building airplanes. Now we are planning commercial flights to outer space.

Our thoughts turn energy into action, attracting to us what we think about. It is not a question of *whether* you can *soar*; the question is how high?

You first need to get clear on what you want in your life and develop a consciousness of **Yes I can!**

Many years ago scientists envisioned exploring beyond our solar system. To that end they launched the spaceship Voyager 1. After a thirty-six-year journey, it became the first manmade object to exit the Earth's solar system, and is still flying. The same Power that created Voyager 1 created you and me. I believe that I can *soar* and you can, too.

You can change your circumstances and those around you by changing your thoughts. First, believe that you can. Belief in the Infinite Power empowers you to harness the powers of the Universe to propel you toward your dreams. It is the creative process, and it is in all our natures to create. I believe we all come to this earth to grow, to expand, and to unfold. "*There is a Power for Good in the Universe and you can use it*," said Ernest Holmes. Belief in this Infinite Power I call Spirit and belief in your dream attract good circumstances to you.

I enjoy living comfortably; however, that is not the source of my joy. My joy comes from within – from Spirit. When you *soar* you do not seek happiness outside of yourself; rather you bring happiness into your life through your thoughts. In doing so, you attract that which you are seeking.

In the book *The Secret,* Rhonda Byrne and co-authors share the impact that the Law of Attraction has on our lives. You attract your good through your thoughts, your belief system. The Master Teacher, Jesus, said, "*It is done unto you as you believe*" (Matthew 8:13). You attract your good not only by your belief, but by your behavior. What comes to us must come through us, through our minds. As Gandhi stated, "*We must* become the change we want to see in the world." It has also been said by many people that if we keep on doing what we've always done, we will get what we've always gotten.

Soaring requires you to take a look at your world-view and what you are attracting. To change your circumstances, change your thinking. If you want more love in your life, become more loving. If you want to receive more, find ways to give more to life and to others.

> I conducted a workshop for a group of individuals who were suffering with brain injuries. Maureen, one of the individuals in the group, shared her recovery strategy. She wanted to get out of the house and at the same time bring more joy to her life. Where and how could she give to her community in order to receive more joy back? She could hardly remember the alphabet due to her injury, so she volunteered with a group of kindergarteners in the school system. This was a great match, as they were unable to judge her abilities. Maureen let go of fear and took the plunge. As a result, she gave and received much love. An amazing thing happened. Maureen's cognitive skills returned so quickly that other members of the group sought volunteer opportunities in the school system as a route to recovery. Maureen's experience demonstrates another universal principle, the Law of Giving and Receiving. What we give to others comes back to us. It also demonstrates the power of love.

Flying on the Wings of Love

What does love have to do with awakening our spirituality? Everything! Love is our connection to Spirit and to other people. "*Love thy neighbor as thy self*," the scriptures tell us (Mark 12:31). It is not only a guiding principle of life, it is a powerful energy exchange, attracting like energy to it. Love attracts love. Love is a basic energy requirement for people who *soar*. Love buoys our spirits and sees the Divine in others. Love allows us to approach life with a sense of openness and willingness to listen to another's perspective, let go of judgment, accept others as they are, and enjoy our differences.

The fourteenth Dalai Lama tells us why love is important to *soaring*:

> *When we feel love and kindness toward others, it not only makes others feel loved and cared for but it helps us also to develop inner happiness and peace.*

People who live life empowered and joyful have a sense of inner peace and happiness. They are kind and giving at the core. How and where do you express caring and giving in your life? The Law of Giving and Receiving tells us that you receive as you give. It is a reciprocal process. How do you show up in the world? What messages are you sending to the Universe? Are you saying, "I am open and ready to receive" or "It's my way or no way?"

What does love feel like to you? What does it mean to you? What connects you to your center? Beautiful music? Spending time with friends? A spiritual service? A jog with your dog? What brings you that inner feeling of peace, love, and connection? Understanding what generates feelings of love and joy in you and putting more of that in your life facilitates *soaring*. Love is empowering.

Our true power comes from our belief in ourselves and our connection to Spirit. Power is the ability to influence the circumstances in our lives; to garner the changes we seek easily and confidently. People who are empowered attract to themselves what they want through their passion, their belief system, and becoming the change they seek. "*Change your thinking, change your life,*" spiritual teachers such as Ernest Holmes and Wayne Dyer tell us. As we change our belief systems, we change, and as a result our worlds change.

Life is energy. Positive energy attracts to us positive results, whereas low-energy thoughts such as fear, anger, and resentment attract in kind. People who *soar* vibrate at higher energy levels. They are confident, open, expectant, and ready to receive. They are also caring and compassionate.

To change your *soaring* altitude, change your attitude and your consciousness. Developing an attitude buoyed by faith and trust in an Infinite Power that always says yes, and that is always attracting to you based on your belief in It, is the wind beneath your wings. Trust and faith in this Infinite Wisdom empowers you to *soar*. In addition to faith and connection to your Higher Power, a *soaring* consciousness is anchored in love.

Developing a *Soaring* Attitude

A **Soaring Attitude** enhances you to reach **Soaring Altitude**. At *soaring* altitude you spend time in silence, envisioning and creating a positive life and sending affirmative thoughts to the Universe. You create your life from moment to moment based on the messages you give yourself and the Universe.

You, like many others, may have noticed that once you focus your attention on an object, it shows up in your life. Let's say you are selecting a new car and are interested in a red one. Soon you'll notice a lot of red cars on the road. Spirit did not suddenly create all those red cars just for you. What you focus on grows; what you give your attention to expands. So if you don't like certain colors, don't give them your attention. Instead, think of your favorite color for your car.

> I once purchased a car for my mother. I went to the dealer and selected a beautiful red car. As I left town I asked the dealer to take the car to my mother's for her approval before finalizing the purchase. The next day I called my mother to find out how she liked the car. Her retort? "Must it be red?" Unwittingly I had selected my favorite color. When the dealer exchanged it for a car in the color of her choice, she was happy.

You are always at choice. You get to choose your destiny. Your destiny is not what someone else wants for you no matter how well-meaning they are. *You* are the captain of your fate – the actor, director, and producer of your life.

Early this morning as I looked out my bedroom window I saw the moon shining brightly and I felt God's presence. As I breathed in the feelings of love and connection, I felt at one with Spirit. Immersed in the Omnipresence, I thought, "What a beautiful day!"

Our minds are always thinking, always chatting. People refer to this as voices in our heads or the "monkey mind" that jumps about without a sense of real direction. You *are not* the voices in your head! You are the one who notices these voices, the observer. Pay attention to the messages you are telling yourself.

Observing your thoughts allows you to change limiting thoughts to positive ones. Thoughts of lack and limitation sap your energy and rob you of your power, whereas positive thoughts uplift and energize you. Within each of us is inner wisdom, an inner guide. It is the navigator on this flight. Your inner guide is your correction device. Replace thoughts of worry, fear, and doubt with positive messages. Your inner thoughts are your guide to *soaring*.

As you awaken to your spiritual essence, recognize that Spirit is within you. Understand that your thoughts become your reality and incorporate this thinking into your life, and your life changes. You begin to believe in yourself and learn to trust the goodness and the abundance of the Universe. Your consciousness expands.

Soaring Practice to Awaken the Spirit Within

> To awaken the spirituality within you, take a deep, slow breath, breathing deep into your heart center, for a count of three. Hold your breath for a count of three and then slowly exhale for a count of three. The very breath you are breathing is the breath of Spirit.
>
> Breathing and connecting with your breath on a regular basis is part of awakening the Spirit within you. Practice this exercise daily for at least five minutes and gradually expand the time as you feel comfortable. As you engage in this practice on an ongoing basis, you connect with your spiritual essence. In future *Flight Lessons* you can expand on and deepen this practice.

Future *Flight Lessons* share additional practices to enhance your *soaring* consciousness. Being clear on your life's purpose, clarifying your vision, and making an action plan for the next steps in your life allow you to *soar* with a sense of direction. With clarity of purpose and a plan to achieve your dreams, practicing gratitude further lifts your consciousness.

Igniting love in your life in *Flight Lesson Six* expands your ability to achieve your goals. As you ignite more love in your life, your enjoyment of life increases. As you apply this *Flight Lesson* in your life, you develop a consciousness of love and become more loving.

A *soaring* consciousness also includes prayer to deepen your communion with the Divine enriching your life. Regular time in meditation also develops your spirituality. With each *Flight Lesson* you experience a new level of awareness, raising your vibrational level. Through forgiveness, you learn to heal old hurts, release old pain, regain your power, and increase your *soaring* altitude.

Change is evitable. Integrating these lessons into your life prepares you for the turbulence you encounter as you *soar*. Adopting self-care as an ongoing aspect of your life is also an important aspect of developing a *soaring* consciousness. Practicing the *soaring* skills in each *Flight Lesson* raises your vibrational level, changes your attitude, and increases your altitude until you *soar* on the wings of faith and find yourself living empowered and joyful.

What is it that you want to do to live in more joy in this moment? Answering that question is an important step to *soaring*, living an empowered lifestyle. It is also a first step in developing a plan to *soar*. In the next *Flight Lesson* you design your own flight plan based on your dreams and expectations.

Applying This *Flight Lesson* in Your Life

Ask yourself:

1. Do I perceive a *Power for Good* operating in my life?

2. What is the source of this power?

3. What am I thinking? What messages do I give myself – positive or negative ones? If my thoughts create my reality, what am I creating?

4. How can I use my creative powers more fully to create the life I want?

Developing Your Flight Plan

Living a Life of Purpose

Your purpose here is to grow and unfold, to live a life of meaning based on your own hopes, desires, and aspirations. Spirit is ever seeking to express through you. It is a call of the Divine – a call to a higher, fuller expression of you and who you came here to be. You can transform your life. Flying safely and joyously requires a plan, one that aligns with your life's purpose.

> From the time I was a young child I was attracted to the helping professions. I wanted to be a psychologist, though it wasn't clear to me what a psychologist was or what they did. What I knew was it was a fancy word for helping people. My mother had been the town's self-proclaimed social worker, providing support and services to families and anyone else who needed it. Her kindness and generosity was well-known throughout the community. It was no surprise that I chose the helping professions; it was in my DNA.

At one point I lost sight of my purpose and got off track. My new goal then was to make money. I left my position in corporate America visiting business expos, and chose a business that I thought would produce the highest income without my direct involvement. I purchased a printing franchise, a skill set out of my expertise. I engaged a partner who managed day-to-day operations so I could focus on marketing and finance.

I hated it! Where was the joy? The people-to-people interaction that I loved so much was gone. The beauty of a perfectly printed work did not equal the joy of assisting in a personal change or facilitating a team success. I didn't like selling; my aim was to give. I was a fish out of water and the business failed. I became ill in the process.

My choice for earning money was out of alignment with my purpose, which was to inspire and motivate individuals and organizations to higher levels of functioning. My ego got in the way of my heart. In hindsight, aligning my passion with my desire to earn money seems so simple. Why not make money doing what you love? Had I asked myself this question, I would have made a different choice.

Spend some quiet time to reflect on where you are in your life and what you want for yourself right now. This is a process that may occur over a period of time. It is an opportunity to check in with your higher self; a time to tap in to your heart center and explore what really gives your life meaning. Think about it. Meditate on it.

What is your life's purpose? What do you want to accomplish on your journey here? What are you passionate about? What gives you joy? What makes your heart sing?

Your purpose speaks to you, and it is what gives meaning to your life. It is what you came here to do or be. As you begin to explore these questions deep within, reasons why you cannot achieve your goal may surface. Ignore them and follow your heart. All those old beliefs are simply issues to address to help you *soar.* As you look at them more closely, reject their validity, and explore the real truth, you develop stronger wings to *soar.*

Since thoughts are things, and you create what you think about, it is important to be clear on what you want to attract into your life. It is important to give the Universe a clear message about what you want to produce. Doing so makes a mold, a picture for the Universe to fill. It gives energy to your dreams and empowers you to realize them – to *soar.*

Envisioning What You Want

> *Visioning is a process, by which we train ourselves to be able to hear, feel, see and catch God's plan for our life.*
> —*Michael Bernard Beckwith, author of* Life Visioning: A Four Stage Evolutionary Journey to Live as Divine Love

The visioning process involves spending time in a meditative state. It is a time of deep surrender and deep listening in which you tap in to your inner self and explore what you want in your life – your passion. Your passion energizes you. It inspires you. It enables you to tap in to your dreams deep within yourself.

You are surrounded by Creative Intelligence, energy vibrations that Dr. Wayne Dyer refers to as *Intention*. When you go within and seek guidance from your higher self, you tap in to your Intention. Your heartbeat resonates with the rhythm of the Universe and you can tune in to the unique plan for your own life. Be willing to listen in the silence and tap in to the wellspring of your own heart to find guidance. It is your passion that fuels the process. Your *Flight Plan* empowers you to *soar.*

> Julie, an educator and program director at a university whose teacher training program was being phased out, used the visioning process to clarify and affirm her next step. Julie said that the process forced her to take an in-depth look at her career for the first time. Working in the high-demand field of math and sciences, she had moved from one position to another on invitation without addressing what she really wanted to do. Julie began to question her entire career. During the process, emotions of fear and feelings of failure arose. Why hadn't she gone to medical school? Was it too late? Visioning, faith, spirituality, and her willingness to ask and answer the deep questions from within led Julie to her own

truth as she sat in contemplation, working through her questions.

Julie determined what she wants the next phase of her life to feel and look like. She has a plan. In the meantime she is content, choosing to play a major role in her family's new business. As a result of the visioning, she is comfortable where she is and trusting the Universe to easily and effortlessly usher in the next phase of her career.

Getting clear on a new plan for your life, or envisioning a new direction, may not be a linear or one-time process.

After my tenure as a professor was finished, I went within to search for direction. But I was not ready to decide what to do next. I simply put in my mind that the right and perfect path would emerge and there was no hurry. One night I awoke with a flood of ideas running through my mind. That was what *soaring* onward and upward looked like for me. My husband suggested that I write them down. I was not interested in getting up in the middle of the night, so I calmly went back to sleep. The next night in the middle of a deep sleep the same thing occurred. This time I got up, went to my computer, jotted down the ideas, and my new venture, Soaring Coaching, was born.

When we ask, *knowing*, the answers come. *Knowing* is faith and belief in your Higher Power, your inner wisdom – that it will safely guide you. When the answer does not come immediately, sit in the silence and imagine what it feels and looks like. Imagination taps in to your heart center, your inner knowing. Eventually the answers you are searching for emerge.

Carly, a successful municipal law attorney, went into a deep hibernation to connect with her highest calling. Carly worked long hours in a downtown high-rise, dressed to the "nines" every day, sat at a computer much of the time, and made a long commute to and from her office week after week. Although Carly loved practicing law, she felt completely stifled by the physical office/city setting. Crying in the morning on her way to work, she was exhausted by the time she got home. Carly just kept going, thinking, "Well, this is what adult life is all about. A nice house, a nice car..." Over time Carly felt like she had become a prisoner to her mortgage – trapped in the American dream. But Carly was not listening to her soul's wisdom; was not listening to her body's wisdom. Carly was sleepwalking through life.

Breast cancer woke Carly up, got her out of her head, and back into her heart, back into her body. Following her diagnosis, Carly went deep inside her soul and rested there for nearly a year – sleeping, meditating, gardening, journaling, dreaming, gardening some more, praying, and listening for her calling.

She came to me for several coaching sessions to help guide her back into alignment with her soul; back into alignment with her body's wisdom. Together we went through many guided visualizations to help Carly capture the feeling, the vibration, and the tone she wanted to regain in her life, which were being energetic, loving, super healthy, joyful, engaged, and working outside! Immediately following her year of hibernation, Carly made several very dramatic changes in her life. She resigned from her high-paying position, sold her home, completed her divorce, and went back to school to obtain a degree in horticulture. Carly is now *soaring* in her new self-guided career, which combines her horticultural background, a certified arborist designation, and her legal experience. She's a tree lawyer!

During our coaching sessions we worked together to reveal and then reframe the limiting beliefs that arose during Carly's meditations and journaling exercises. In particular, "I'm too old to start over" and "I'm a woman; who will hire me?" played havoc with her goals. With practice and self-discipline, Carly was able to reframe these limiting beliefs into "I'm a trailblazer! There are thousands of women starting over at my age. I'm on the cutting edge! Who cares how old I am, I feel great! I am *soaring*!"

Letting Go of Limiting Beliefs

Sometimes as we envision, negative thoughts and beliefs surface. All the reasons *not* to move forward surface rather than the reasons to proceed. Since beliefs are the filters through which we view the world, our beliefs can support or limit our getting what we want in life. Underlying thoughts regarding your ability and self-worth can be positive or negative, and sometimes false. It is important to identify false beliefs as part of your visioning process.

When reasons "why not" arise, examine their validity and replace them with positive thoughts. Shine the light of truth on them and recognize them for what they are, usually fear and resistance. As these limiting beliefs surface, write down affirmative beliefs to negate them, and read those statements daily. Immerse yourself in the new belief until your subconscious mind accepts it. Visualization and affirmations discussed in *Flight Lesson Four* are ways to refute false beliefs and instill new ones. With clarity of direction you move forward, more powerfully positioned to *soar*.

Dreaming Big

Meanwhile, dream big! Build the mental mindset to *soar* by *expecting* your dream to materialize in a big way by thinking big.

> My friend Patricia demonstrates this practice daily. She says, "I don't want a little bit of anything!" That is her mantra. Sharing and giving are her vehicles.

With a heart of gold she gives to life in a big way, and at the same time makes large demands on the Universe, and the Universe responds in kind. She generously gives of her time, talent, and treasure to various community organizations and is very prosperous. She lives in a *big house* and drives a *big car.* She wears *big jewelry* and *flowing garments.* She has devoted her life to family, community service, and her church, always giving *big,* primarily of herself, with great enthusiasm. She has a *big* smile; a *big,* hearty laugh; and lights up the world wherever she is. She doesn't go to the doctor, is never sick, and always finds a way to *Give* to others with a capital *G.* I am attracted to her loving ways and her giving-ness. She is a living example of building a mental prototype of what you want your world to be like.

What mental picture are you building? Perhaps like Vera you want to be an Olympian, or like Carly you want to move into a totally new career. You now seek to serve humanity in a different way by doing something that makes your heart sing and brings joy to every waking moment.

My talented hair stylist had a small beauty salon in south-central Los Angeles. She wanted to make a larger impact on the beauty industry. We decided to exchange services. In exchange for her styling my hair, I would coach her to dream big and make an action plan to implement her dreams. As a result she opened a full-service salon offering a wide range of personal care services in a more highly desirable location, taught hair design, and created a product line of instructional materials. Today she is running another business while maintaining an income stream from her salon.

Think big regarding the quality of the life you want for yourself. I am not talking about your material possessions, but if things are important to you, put them on the list. As you picture your dream life, event, or goal, pay attention to the mental pictures you are building. What actions will you take?

Dr. Martin Luther King Jr. dreamed of a world free of inequality. Belief in his dream moved him from humble beginnings to the world stage. Soon women and men, people with disabilities, gays and lesbians, hitched their wagons to the same dream, and the world as we knew it changed forever, garnering him a Nobel Peace Prize.

As a high school freshman, I dreamed big. I loved the band and wanted to be a head majorette as they led the band through my small town before Friday evening football games. What excitement! They also led the band onto the field to display the school colors before football games and for the half-time extravaganza. There were several baton twirlers marching in step with the band. "Why bring up the rear when you can be number one?" That was my goal. That was how I saw myself, leading the band, blowing the whistle, and calling the plays. Sheer joy!

No one told me that African-American girls were unwelcome as head majorettes at that time. So full of energy and enthusiasm, I practiced for the tryouts and was not chosen. The quiet buzz going through the school asked why I would even try. Undaunted, I took my baton everywhere. Daily I practiced. I strutted to school. I twirled on the way home. I practiced after school. I was never far from my baton. I exchanged my lightweight baton for one with the proper weight and balance for me. All year I lived and breathed marching with the band as a majorette. When tryouts came around again, yes, you guessed it; I made history in that school and was first runner-up for homecoming queen.

You, too, can break through barriers – the ones in your mind as well as those in the minds of others as to what you can and cannot do. Build a mental picture of what you want to accomplish, mentally practice seeing yourself in that role daily, and see the goal accomplished in your mind. Just as mental practice is important in sports, it is important in our lives.

I took my first golf lesson at the La Costa Resorts in Carlsbad, California. A friend who played golf was visiting and scheduled a lesson for me. I was excited to learn from a pro, only to find out that my very first lesson was to sit in a room and watch an electronic illumination of the golf swing. The purpose behind this type of training was to learn to move through the proper swing without conscious thought. I had to build new neural pathways for the golf swing. Therefore, my first practice at playing golf was truly in my mind.

After a tennis serve, the server automatically moves into position to receive the return. This habit is built into the brain/body coordination through practice. *Soaring* is learning to move through life intuitively, joyfully, and empowered, without struggle.

My life's mate, my beloved husband, had transitioned to eternity, leaving me to build a new life as an independent single woman. While moving through this dark night of the soul experience, one day I received a sweepstake packet in the mail with a picture of a pair of hairy male hands declaring on the outside of the envelope, "*I, Matti Dobbs, Am a Winner.*" "Indeed she is," I thought as I immediately cut out the hands and pasted them on the center of my mirror as a daily reminder that *I, Matti Dobbs, am a winner.* This to me was a sign from the Universe reminding me of the truth.

You can create your own reminders. You can set goals and build your own mental images. Empowered and in charge of what happens in your life, you can send messages to the Universe and your subconscious mind regarding your desires.

Developing Your *Flight Plan*

Your *Flight Plan* is a transformational tool to *soar*. It is your personal "blueprint for success," and expresses your desires and wishes. These desires and wishes are your goals. Developing your *Flight Plan* involves five steps:

I.   Visioning: Asking yourself what you really want to do with your life now

II. Listening to your inner wisdom and setting goals

III. Prioritizing your goals

IV. Designing an action plan to carry out your goals

V.   Taking action to implement your plan

I. Visioning: Asking Yourself Questions

1. Find a quiet, comfortable place to contemplate the next phase in your life. Have pen and paper available to record your answers. During a period of reflection ask yourself the following question: "What is my passion?" To help you answer this question, think about what energizes you and what you really enjoy doing. What is yours to do?

2. "What is my purpose?" To help you answer this question, ask yourself:

   a. Why am I here?

b. Who did I come here to be?

c. What did I come here to do?

d. Am I doing it?

e. What would I like to be doing?

3. From your answers write a purpose statement for your life.

4. Now ask yourself, "With my purpose and passion in mind, what is my vision for my life?"

a. What is next for me to do?

b. What does it look like?

c. What does it feel like?

d. What obstacles or limiting beliefs hinder my vision?

e. What actions can I take to overcome obstacles or limiting beliefs?

II. Listening to Your Inner Wisdom and Setting Goals

In the quietness, listen to your heart's desires. Your inner wisdom will give you the answers. Your desires and dreams are goals. Write broad statements about what you desire to do to achieve your purpose and vision. Set aside time daily to work on your visioning until you reach clarity.

1.

2.

3.

III. Prioritizing Your Goals

When you feel that your list is complete, prioritize your goals based on their order of importance to you.

1.

2.

3.

IV. Designing Your Action Plan

An action plan identifies the actual steps you will take to implement your plan. It answers the questions: "What will I do?" "How will I do it?" and "When will I start?" And asking "Who?" identifies what resources are needed to carry out your plan. Using the Action Plan below as a guide, identify the steps required to implement your *Flight Plan. Consider designating an entire notebook to this visioning process, incorporating the questions in this Flight Lesson.*

My *Soaring Flight Plan*

Goal:

What	How	Who	When
1.			
2.			
3.			
4.			
5.			

Goal:

What	How	Who	When
1.			
2.			
3.			
4.			
5.			

Goal:

What	How	Who	When
1.			
2.			
3.			
4.			
5.			

V. Taking Action

You have reached the action phase of your plan. It is now time to schedule your action steps into your calendar. For example, a first step for you may involve collecting additional information, so identifying and scheduling the time on your calendar to collect information is an appropriate action step for you. Your *Flight Plan* is fluid. As you continue your *Flight Lessons* you may learn about information and tools to enhance your plan. As you explore these tools your *Flight Plan* may also change.

Future *Flight Lessons* share *soaring* practices to facilitate achieving your goals easily and comfortably. The next *Flight Lesson* provides practices for internalizing your plan and incorporating it as an active part of your daily life.

Applying This *Flight Lesson* in Your Life

1. Your *Flight Plan* is your planning tool for *soaring*. Take action and monitor your progress on your *Flight Plan* periodically.

2. As you explore new *Flight Lessons,* change your plan as needed.

FLIGHT LESSON FOUR

Visualize It! Picture It! Affirm It!

Visualizing to Create the Life You Want

Your *Flight Plan* is your personal blueprint to create what you want in your life. As a result of the last *Flight Lesson,* you are clear on your purpose, you are clear on your goals, and you have a vision for the next phase of the journey.

Since our thoughts fuel our attitudes and approaches to life, we are creating our experiences one thought at a time. We can change any condition in our lives through the power of our minds. Your thoughts tap in to the universal flow of life and create that which you are seeking. You can use your mind to create the next step in your transformation.

Mentally sending images to Spirit changes your world-view, and as your world-view changes your circumstances change. This *Flight Lesson* focuses on changing your consciousness to *Yes I can!* Creative visualization is a tool to consciously create the life you want through your imagination. Daydream! Imagine!

Believe It! See It! Feel It! Create It!

Live daily in the reality of your vision. That's the way creative visualization works. You are always creating, consciously or unconsciously, so why not create what you want? Energy attracts like energy. The Law of Attraction attracts to you what you think about, and your thoughts imprint your next step upon the Universe. You have done this all your life consciously or unconsciously. Now I invite you to consciously move toward your dreams.

Let's go back to the intention you set in *Flight Lesson Three*. Imagine what it looks like. Visualize its implementation. Paint a picture in your mind of what you want to create and visualize it daily. Create a vision board to pictorially depict your intention. Write an affirmation to support your dream. Visualize it! Picture it! Affirm it!

In her book *Creative Visualization*, Shakti Gawain identifies four basic steps for creative visualization:

1. Identify what you would like to realize or manifest in your life – a change of events, state of mind or conditions, a relationship issue, or something else.

2. Create a clear picture, idea, or situation that you want to achieve.

3. Focus on your idea or picture it clearly and frequently in a relaxed manner.

4. Give it positive energy. Affirm the outcome you desire. See the goal completed with joy and positive emotions. Picture yourself enjoying your accomplishments.

    From the time I was a child I wanted to help people make their lives better. That guiding light has directed my career. Dreams, visualization, and the Law of Attraction guided me to my next thing to do, although I must admit that it was not the concentrated, directed energy with conviction that I am now suggesting to you. I kept my dreams in the back of my mind and in my spirit in a steady, relaxed manner. With my inner light and spiritual guidance system, I *soared* with minimal turbulence and moved steadily toward my goals.

Your dreams can guide you to the next step in your life. Directed thought sends a message to your subconscious mind as well as to the Universe. Coupled with *soaring* practices such as prayer and meditation, creative visualization can help you move toward your dreams easily and comfortably. Here's how it works:

    Lisa Nichols, renowned motivational speaker and author of six bestselling books, credits creative visualization with changing her life from a welfare recipient to an international motivational speaker for groups and corporations. At one of her seminars, Lisa informed us that she would sit in bed at night and visualize.

Each morning she focused on her dream to motivate thousands through the power of her word. In front of her bathroom mirror, she spoke to thousands of people with tearful emotions. She gave the same speech over and over to thousands in her mind. She painted a picture of what life looked like for her as a motivational speaker and played that tape in her head constantly. At the same time she took action steps to move toward her dream. Now she is literally speaking to and motivating thousands of people as she lives the dream she painted in her mind.

You, too, can realize your dreams easily and comfortably. Build a mental picture of the goal you want to accomplish – a new job, personal development, new acquisition, changed relations, whatever you want in your life. Daily set aside time to picture what you want in your mind, as long as it is life-affirming. You cannot manipulate or change others or achieve negative ends. Focus on a positive you want in your own life.

Practice daily. See your dream realized in your own mind, fully accomplished! Bask in it! Revel in it! Feel it! Visualize and dream, realizing the vision in your *Flight Plan.* Put the full power of your emotions behind it and you will realize it!

Dr. Wayne Dyer, author of *You'll See It When You Believe It*, reminds us that creative visualization works because our actions come from our vision, and that everything we do is based on the pictures we put in our minds. There is no such thing as failure because whatever we are attempting to accomplish is already here; we can only produce results. He suggests that we be willing to do whatever it takes to make it happen, and our actions will produce results.

Picture It!

Along with your daily visualization you may choose to create a vision board, treasure map, or artistic representation of your vision. Vision-boarding, or treasure-mapping, is using colorful graphics, pictures from magazines, and/or computer printouts to build a picture of what you want in your life... your dreams. It is a powerful way to support the consciousness of both the quality and outcomes you want in your life. In my office I have a colorful vision board of events and qualities I want in my life. It has pictures of places to travel; healthy food; symbols of prosperity; words to inspire me such as *Love, Family, Balance, Joy*; an image of this book; and other reminders of what I desire to create in my life. My niece carries a picture of her vision board on her cell phone for daily reference. What a wonderful reminder, wherever you are, at work or play.

> I conducted a series of workshops for women in alcoholic recovery. Vision-boarding was one of the transformational tools to help the women build pictures of their desired future. Along with "wisdom cards" of affirmations that I gave them each week, their vision boards were reminders that we set dreams in motion with our thoughts. We affirm them by our behavior. In those workshops, not only did

we create mental images of what could be through pictures and daily affirmations, each woman celebrated herself for her accomplishments and where she was in life at that moment – in the process of a major transformation. Her vision board was a daily reminder of her goals. Each woman displayed her vision board, shared the affirmations she had carefully chosen, and proudly told her story and where she was in her journey. Although the long-term results of this process were not measured, pre- and post-test responses were positive, and if we believe the Law of Cause and Effect, thoughts of the mind produce in kind. These vision boards imprinted on each woman's mind her personal goals and what was possible for her.

Building vision boards also created excitement and planning for a group of thirty-five inner-city high school girls in a leadership development program. This target group of young women were juniors and seniors preparing to graduate and plan for the next phase of their lives. Creating vision boards was a way for them not only to plan, but to take away a picture of what life could be like for them. A sense of excitement and high energy filled the room as they worked together, dreaming and cutting out pictures. During our time together they were able to imagine, dream, and create what life would be like for them as they graduated and prepared for the next step in their lives. Each girl left with a collage, a picture of her vision in living color to display and guide her future.

Creating a picture of your dream raises your energy level. It helps you *soar* to a new level of expectations for yourself. It also communicates to your subconscious that you are serious about your dream and that you are ready to *soar*. It serves as a quick mental check-in with yourself. Your eye/brain communication quickly tells you where you are in relation to achieving the results you want.

I used vision-boarding when I conducted a series of three-day diversity workshops for law enforcement officers. They were divided into teams that used vision boards to graphically depict ways different groups could coalesce around common goals, as well as to provide positive images of their key learnings about different cultural groups. Although some participants initially used caricatures to depict racist stereotypes, most of the groups fully embraced the exercise as a way to learn about other cultures, and prepared group collages of what real diversity teamwork could look like in their organization. Pre- and post-tests demonstrated changes in the overall attitudes of participants during the training. I believe that vision boards were a non-threatening way for officers to embrace diversity and envision new images of creating a harmonious work life.

Building visuals of desired positive change speaks to your subconscious as well as your conscious mind. Looking at your vision board daily sends a message to the Universe as well as reminding your conscious mind to work on achieving your goals. It engenders positive feelings, and often without conscious thought you begin to move in the direction of your goals.

Affirm It!

Affirmations are positive statements about what you want to manifest in your life. Affirming what you want to see in your life is another practice to support your vision and create your reality. Sending statements to your subconscious mind changes the way you view the world, and as your world-view changes, the circumstances in your world also change.

I use affirmations daily to change my thinking and send a positive message to the Universe about what I expect. When I arise in the morning I begin each day with an expression of gratitude: *Thank you, Spirit, for this day*.

Sometimes I affirm, *This is the day Spirit has made. I am happy and rejoicing in it!* Or *Spirit, I am an instrument of peace.*

During periods of grief, while I was on my beach walks with the sun shining brightly on the ocean and sparkling on crystals of sand, my heart was aching. I daily reminded myself of the truth: *There's a rainbow at the end of this tunnel! One day this pain will go away! There's light at the end of this tunnel!* I walked and affirmed with emotion and conviction.

During that dark period I developed a health issue. Daily I sat on my sofa, looked out my window, and affirmed: *I am healthy, whole, and complete. I am energetic and healthy.* Even today when confronted with a negative situation, I affirm: *This, too, shall pass!*

When I get in my car I say, *God guides the journey.* My favorite affirmation for handling a circumstance such as dental treatment is to affirm the Divine Presence within me: *God and I are one!* I also use: *There is sunshine in the rain.*

You see, life always affords us *opportunity*; opportunity to enjoy a positive experience or heal a negative one. We are always at choice. Although we may not always get to choose our experiences, we do get to affirm our reactions to them. My mother always said, "Name it and claim it!"

Invite more peace, love, and prosperity into your life by naming and claiming what you want through the power of your word. Choose each day to claim your experiences through positive affirmations.

> I met Gwen after she recently moved to California and worked from home in a rental property. Although a homeowner in another state, she doubted her ability to purchase a home in California. I sent Gwen an affirmation that she posted on her refrigerator:

Today I am empowered to reach my highest possibilities. I now move forward into my greatest good, Divinely directed and lavishly prospered. My vision fills me with a realization of God's strength, power, and abundance that have always been mine. I claim them now!

She affirmed the reading daily. One day she called and told me, "I am a new homeowner and I want to thank you for the affirmation you sent." Although the affirmation was not Gwen's words, she embraced them and affirmed them daily. Her affirmation manifested in her life.

Your visualizations, pictorial images, and affirmations will not only manifest in your life, they will help you *soar*. Now that you have learned how to mentally attract what you want in your life, it is time to develop a consciousness – a mindset to help you realize your dreams. Begin with igniting love in the next *Flight Lesson*.

Applying This *Flight Lesson* in Your Life

1. **Visualize it.** Rewrite your vision/goal from your *Flight Plan* in *Flight Lesson Three* on a card and place it in an easily accessible place where you can see it often. Create a clear picture in your mind of your goal accomplished exactly the way you want it to be. Mentally see it in your mind often. Feel the emotions associated with your dream. Feel the joy, revel in your accomplishment, and

enjoy the realization of your dream in your mind daily.

2. **Picture it**. Build a collage to support your vision/ goal or something you would like to experience in your life. Cut out words and pictures from magazines; find them on a computer; use advertisements, brochures, or draw them yourself. Create a picture of what you want to show up in your life. Feel all the emotions associated with the realization of your vision in your life. You may choose to create a scrapbook or booklet. Do whatever works for you. Put the Universe on notice that you are ready to change your circumstances… now! Look at your collage daily. Relax and detach from a specific way that your dream will show up. Simply expect it. Enjoy the accomplishment of your dream in your mind.

3. **Affirm it.** Your *Flight Plan* is an active guide to *soaring*. Write positive statements to support your vision/goal or anything you want to occur in your life, small or large. Repeat these statements and incorporate them into your daily life as an ongoing way to live. For example, "This is a beautiful day!" Use these statements as a way to frame your day, deter fear, allay anxiety, or realize your goals. Expect the best no matter the circumstances.

FLIGHT LESSON FIVE

Igniting Love

*God is love: and whoever dwells in Love
dwells in God, and God dwells in them.*
        —1 John 4:16

God is Love. The entire Universe is made of Love. Love is the energy for your flight, the power source that enables you to *soar*. Igniting love raises your spirits and causes you to vibrate at a higher energy level.

Deep within each of us is a longing, a burning desire for love and connection. It is the call of the Divine. Spirit is ever seeking to express through you; to ignite the love within you; to awaken you to your own spirituality, your own inherent nature. Igniting love is awakening your spiritual essence.

Kabir Helminski, in *The Knowing Heart*, tells the story of a little fish who learned that without water he would die. Alarmed, he went to tell his mother of the urgent need for water. "Water, my dear, that's what we are swimming in," said his mother. You and I are like that little fish swimming in an ocean of love, yet often we're enmeshed in the activities of daily living and fail to recognize it.

Love is incarnate within us. Watching the stars on a clear night, looking at the majesty of an ice glacier in Alaska, standing on the beach at Maui, enthralled in the beauty of a waterfall on Kauai, watching the sunset on the California shore, and meditating while walking during a snowstorm in the Colorado mountains all ignite my inner Spirit. Have you seen color photographs of new stars and planets forming in outer space? The spectacular beauty of these images also touches my heart.

To ignite love, observe this beauty with more than your eyes. Look deep from within your heart center. Love is the power to see and feel with all of your senses. It is available in abundant supply, yet many of us feel isolated and alone. We seek love outside of ourselves, often looking for someone else to fill the void, to fix or complete what we feel is missing within ourselves. Love is within; it is an inside job.

Research shows that people who give and receive love are happier and have a 50 percent increased chance of longevity. However, the greatest benefits for longevity and well-being come not from receiving love, but from *giving* it to others. (Research conducted by Dr. Emma Seppala, Director of the Center for Compassion and Altruism Research and Education at Stanford University, April 28, 2013). Corroborating studies suggest that connecting with others in a meaningful way helps us enjoy improved mental and physical health and better immune function.

Love is a gift, a gift of Spirit. It's our Divine inheritance. We can open our hearts and share our gifts anytime we choose and make ourselves happier. The question is how do you open to love? How do you ignite the love within you?

For many it is simply a part of life – it just is. It comes easily and naturally. For others love is a decision, one to consciously live in the fullness of Spirit, to embrace their divinity. We have free will and can make a choice about the quality of life we choose to live.

> I met a young couple who literally glowed with love and happiness. I was attracted to their inner light; soft, gentle smiles; and eyes aglow with happiness. Sheila was in a wheelchair, and her husband, Ron, was her caregiver. He pushed her wheelchair everywhere and assisted with many of her daily requirements. After watching their interaction over a period of time, I asked them to share with me the reason for their happiness, particularly in light of Sheila's health issue.
>
> Ron shared that as a young boy he had attended church with his family, and although his father attempted to discuss the service with him, he did not understand the ritual. He did not feel that he received value, and upon becoming an adult, he stopped attending any church. As a young working man, he was the least-respected employee in the firm as a project manager. Management complained about his performance; he resisted in complying, which resulted in creating a contentious relationship.

One day Ron made the decision to interrupt the cycle and view the entire situation with love. He decided to stop resisting, do the best job he knew how, and if he got fired, so be it. Instead, the entire atmosphere changed at his workplace. He rose from the least to the most valued employee. He attributed these changes in performance and relationships to his own change in attitude. Ron made a decision to bring love and happiness to his personal life. "Love is within you. You have to look within yourself to find it," he said.

Sheila attributed her glow to having worked through years of pain and reaching the decision that she could live a life of pain and misery, or one of love. Turning away from her physical condition, she chose not to name her disease. "It doesn't matter what they call it." What mattered, she said, was her reaction to it. After years of pain, medications, and numerous doctors, her decision was to handle it all with love. She and Ron appeared joyously happy as they smiled and looked at each other and the world with love.

When love, the universal magnet, is brought into action in the consciousness of our race, it will change all our methods of supplying human wants. It will harmonize all the forces of nature and will dissolve the

discords that now infest earth and air...The earth shall yet be made paradise by the power of love.

—H. Emilie Cady

Imagine a world filled with love, free of power and conflict. What would life be like if each of us became a committee of one to make that happen? You have the power to change your world right where you are right now. Since your thoughts create your experiences, set an intention to begin in this moment to be a loving presence in the world to activate love in all your affairs. Love is a decision.

If you have no idea what this means, imagine what it is, what it feels like, what it looks like in your mind, to be residing in a state of love. Is this the type of world you want to live in?

Set an intention to be a loving presence in the world in your daily activities. Maybe you choose to hold the door open for someone behind you, relinquish your spot to someone else waiting in line at the train station, smile at the grocery clerk, exercise flexibility in a business transaction, pet your dog, or be fully present with your family at the dinner table. You might take your staff out to lunch or create a more humane workplace with life-affirming incentives. Perhaps you could extend a helping hand to a friend or someone in need. How do you begin? Think, feel, speak, and act as love.

Prayer of Saint Francis

My intent is to love – every day. This beautiful prayer attributed to Saint Francis was an early starting point for me to consciously practice loving:

> *Lord make me an instrument of thy peace.*
> *Where there is hatred let me sow love;*
> *Where there is injury, pardon;*
> *Where there is doubt, faith;*
> *Where there is despair, hope;*
> *Where there is darkness, light;*
> *Where there is sadness, joy.*

I said the first two lines for years until this occurred to me one day: *I am an instrument of Peace. I am love.*

Affirming this daily helps me instill in my consciousness that I am love. Now I say frequently, *God's Love and Light are shining through me. I am love in action.*

In *A Return to Love*, Marianne Williamson said, *"Love takes more than crystals and rainbows, it takes discipline and practice. It's not just a sweet sentiment from a Hallmark card. It is a radical commitment to a different way of being, a mental response to life that is completely at odds with the rest of the world."*

Begin by connecting with your higher self, the Divine Presence within. In silence, meditate on love to ignite and embody love within you.

Meditation for Igniting Love Within

Take a deep breath and exhale deeply. As you inhale, imagine love permeating every cell of your being. Exhale slowly and deliberately. Continue to breathe in love, filling your entire being and exhaling slowly. Fill your heart, your mind, every organ, and your spirit with love. After filling your own spirit, mentally send love to friends, loved ones, and the Universe. Sit in the silence, affirming this truth, allowing each breath to guide you deeper into feelings of love. Set aside time daily to practice igniting the love within you through this meditation.

Setting a Love Intention

Setting a love intention is a great way to begin your day. Each morning before getting out of bed I express gratitude for the love and light that shines as me. I set the intention early in my day. When I act out of intention I remind myself of my love intent, reaffirm my intention, and change my behavior.

Recently I had trouble with my computer. When the third technical support representative appeared on the line to assist me, rather than succinctly telling him the nature of the problem, I found myself telling him about the previous lack of success I'd experienced with the other two representatives. When I noticed that I was complaining, I stopped, recognizing this new source of support, and shared the nature of the problem. I let go of the need to express frustration and decided to be love in action. It worked more effectively, and after a new backup system was installed, my computer worked perfectly.

What does love have to do with it? Love does not judge, blame, or complain. Love lifts others and energizes you to *soar.* Make a decision to ignite love in all your activities.

Loving and Appreciating Yourself

Begin by loving yourself. Give yourself all the tender loving care that you want someone else to give you. You can give that love to yourself daily in the way you treat yourself. Be kind to yourself. Give yourself positive feedback and support. Speak nicely to yourself. Use positive affirmations to support and encourage yourself.

Practicing Mirror Talk

Louise Hay, in her book *You Can Heal Your Life,* suggests using "mirror talk" as a practice to begin loving yourself. Look in the mirror, look past any imperfection, shower yourself with love, and give yourself positive feedback. Look into your own eyes and say, "I love you! I am beautiful!" If you find this difficult to do, *imagine* yourself looking into the mirror until you are able to actually do this in reality. I also use mirror talk as an ongoing practice to check in with the little girl who lives inside of me, to talk to her, be kind to her, and make sure that she is okay. It is a wonderful way to love and nurture you.

Sending Yourself Positive Messages

Write yourself a love note and post it on your mirror. Write yourself a love letter to encourage yourself when you are feeling down. I have a friend who places love notes in strategic places around the house to remind herself of love's positive power.

Being Loving

There was a time in my life when I looked to others for love. My husband, the love of my life, had passed on to a new reality. I felt alone and sought the comfort of friends and relatives. I looked for many ways to fill the void. I made a conscious choice to make each day a positive one grounded in love energy.

I put love energy into the Universe in every way that I could in my daily activities – walking the beach, in workshops, in classes, and spending quality time with family and friends. Every day, in every way, I intuitively tried to spread the love to others that I wanted for myself. In so doing, I healed myself and helped heal others.

It was my own inner drive and need for love and connection that motivated me. It is in the giving that we receive. If we want more love in our lives, rather than looking for the other person to fill that need, we can become more loving and give love to ourselves and others.

Love will come back to us. We can reach into the storehouse of love deep within and fill our own vessels from the reservoir of our own spirits. Giving love will help us attract, create, and sustain more love. That's a tall order when we feel depleted ourselves. An essential ingredient in establishing loving relationships is recognition of our oneness with Spirit. Sometimes we have to return to Universal Love to get replenished and feel love.

Stephanie Sorensen said in her book *Unlimited Visibility,* "*When we are steadfast in our acknowledgment of oneness with God, we do not look to the world as the source of our love; we look within to that eternal Wellspring of Life that is always pouring forth the aliveness we seek.*"

Sit in the quiet and breathe deeply to feel your oneness with Spirit. Prayer and meditation discussed in future *Flight Lessons* are ways to accomplish this.

Creating Loving Relationships

When we give and receive love, we create loving relationships. We know from quantum physics that when we interact with another entity we change the nature of that entity as a result of our interaction. Quantum physics helps us recognize that we can change the quality of our relationships. Through our thoughts we can create, nurture, and sustain love. Our core beliefs about ourselves, people, love, and relationships impact the nature of our relationships. What we think about we bring about. We are all connected.

Changing Your Perspective

When you meet acrimony and negativity, take the time to change your perspective. A new perspective is to see the other person not as a threat but as someone in fear or needing love. When we change our perspectives we are able to change our negative thoughts to ones of love.

I have found that when I stop trying to fix the other person or fix the relationship, and instead extend love, the relationship changes. Our thoughts create our experiences.

> I found this to be true in the early days of Jane's marriage. As Jane and her husband worked out the relationship between themselves, two independent professionals with diverse careers, there were times that a lack of communication sounded like blah, blah, blah – endless babbling. Tired of hearing the blah, blah blahs, Jane decided that she would leave the marriage at the end of the teaching semester and relocate to another residence. She hired a realtor and began to search for a new home in an area close to her family. Meanwhile she made the decision to be the most loving person she could and relinquish all demands on her new husband. She genuinely loved

him; she was simply tired of the blah, blah, blahs. She relinquished all demands and instead focused on being love. When the semester ended, their relationship had changed. As she showed more love, she received more love. It is truly in the giving that we receive.

We attract what we give. Our thoughts about others directly affect the nature of our relationships with them. We are all one. We are interconnected. We are each co-creators of our relationships. What are you thinking about your loved ones? Are the thoughts judgmental, angry, or critical? These thoughts impact our relationships and what we receive in return.

Henry Grayson, as he relates in *Mindful Loving,* conducted an experiment that illustrates this relationship. For one month he vacillated daily between positive and negative thoughts about his wife. On the days when he thought negatively about his wife, he received negative reactions from her. On days when he thought positive thoughts, he found his wife receptive and loving. He attributed changes in her behavior to his positive or negative thoughts about her.

Our thoughts impact the nature and quality of our relationships. We can change relationships negatively or positively with our thoughts whether we openly express them or not. Just as thoughts of love cause plants to grow more hardily, and positive words written on bottles of water created beautiful images in Dr. Masaru Emoto's research as reported in *The True Power of Water, 2003,* loving thoughts can help your relationships grow more robustly. He said:

We consistently found that water responded to positive words by creating beautiful crystals. As if it wanted to express its joyous feelings, the crystals opened up like a flower. In contrast when water was shown negative words it did not form crystals.

Thinking negatively about yourself, your mate, or your significant other impacts the quality of your relationship even when you don't actively express it. Judgmental and critical thoughts generate relationships characterized by judgment and resentment. What we put out is what we get back. Ralph Waldo Emerson refers to this as the Law of Compensation.

If you want more love, put more love into the Universe and express love in your relationships. What are you thinking as you move about your daily life? Are your thoughts judgmental, angry, or critical? Make a decision to express more love.

It can be difficult to express love when we are feeling wounded or fearful and have no understanding of what unconditional love is. Often we go looking for love from others to heal the lack of real love in our own lives – perhaps the love we feel we didn't get from our mother, father, or others significant to us in our formative years. Rather than giving love unconditionally, we look to others to meet our needs, often making ourselves victims dependent on someone else who may not be experienced in loving. Now is your opportunity to love and nurture that little girl or boy yearning for love deep within you. Give yourself the unconditional love that you want others to give you.

If you find this difficult, practice, practice, practice! The most important practice is your spiritual practice. Spiritual practices consist of activities that nurture your wholeness and well-being. This is when you take the time to acknowledge your connection to Spirit and get in touch with your own divinity, the Spirit within you. Practice takes many forms, such as in the love meditation discussed above. Expressing love is an important spiritual practice to nurture your well-being and relationships and to ignite love within.

Expressing Love in Your Work

The person who was able to be most helpful to me when I suffered from whiplash was a man whose hands had been crushed in a car accident. He vowed that when his hands were healed he would heal others in return. He is more than a massage therapist; he expresses love daily in his work.

Becoming a Love Ambassador

A love ambassador is someone with a clear intent to be an emissary of love. Think, feel, speak, and act as love itself. When the opportunity arises in your daily life, choose to be loving and kind. Express unconditional caring to others. Unconditional love is love based on giving unselfishly. Perform random acts of kindness and brighten someone's day with no expectation of reciprocity.

> My mother was a love ambassador. She had a very clear intention to express love. This was her purpose. She called it her

"motto," and expressed it often: "*If I can do anything, say a kind word or do a kind deed to help someone on their way, my living won't be in vain.*" Daily she consciously lived the reality of her purpose until the age of ninety-four, brightening the life of anyone she met with her love and wisdom. Her doctors shared how she inspired them. Although they were the professional healers, in many ways she reversed the roles, giving them as much as they gave her. Her life, dedicated to loving and giving to others, substantiates the research on love, longevity, and happiness.

Igniting love lays a strong foundation for *you to soar.* Awakening to your spiritual essence that is love, igniting the love within you, and sharing it with others generates more love in your life. As your love expands and grows, you, too, expand and grow. Your world changes and expands. New opportunities arise. New possibilities occur. "Open your Heart and Let Your Love Flow Free," as sung by Washantura. A whole new world-view awaits you. As love in action, you are poised to *soar.*

Applying This *Flight Lesson* in Your Life

1. Loving yourself is a good place to ignite the love within you. Write yourself a love letter telling yourself all the things you like about yourself. Post your letter where you can remind yourself of your strengths.

2. State the things you love about yourself in positive affirmations. For example, say, "I am kind and loving." Write them in your journal or post them around the house to remind yourself often.

3. Expressing love to others benefits your health and happiness. Become a love ambassador. Set a daily intention to express unconditional love to others in your life. Give love for the joy of it and increase your own joy.

4. When you find yourself expressing an emotion other than love, stop! Reframe the conversation from one that judges or puts down the other person to one that gives unconditional love.

5. As you intentionally express love for love's sake, observe the impact of your new behavior on your own attitude as well as on the world around you. Keep a journal of any changes you observe.

6. Make a *Love Action Plan*. Include in it a list of things you are willing to do to ignite more love in your life.

My Love Action Plan

Goal:

What	How	Who	When
1.			
2.			
3.			
4.			
5.			

Goal:

What	How	Who	When
1.			
2.			
3.			
4.			
5.			

Lifting Off with Gratitude

Living in the Magnificence

Come *soar* with me. I live in the Omnipresence. I walk and talk with God every day. I have a passionate relationship with Spirit. My waking prayer is "Thank You, Thank You, Spirit." I look at what's great in my life and ways to make it work more effectively to bring me joy based on my interests and values. Before going to bed at night my attention again turns to gratitude. Living in this consciousness of gratitude and connection gives me joy.

Soaring is living in the Magnificence, loving, and appreciating life. This morning as I was brushing my teeth I saw in my mirror the beautiful reflection of a scarlet sun rising over the treetops of my neighbor's home. Breathing a deep sigh of gratitude I thought, "How great Thou art! How grateful I am to live in this beautiful world." My spirits soared with gratitude.

Soaring is living in this state of bliss 24/7. It is seeing God everywhere, in all things, and recognizing the beauty in all things. It is conscious awareness and appreciation for life; conscious awareness that **God is** *and* **I am** an individualized expression of this Magnificence. Thinking and believing this way attracts to me even more of this beautiful life.

> Today I purchased a case of printer paper from the store. It was relatively simple to move it from the shelf down into my shopping cart. But when I sought to lift it from the cart into my car, it felt heavier. I paused. As I did so, another shopper pulled his truck closer and signaled to me. Thinking he wanted to pass I pulled my cart closer to my car. The man got out of his truck, picked the box up out of my cart, and put it in my trunk. Gratitude always brings more goodness into your life.

Gratitude is healing energy, a balm that can heal perceptions of lack or limitation. Gratitude focuses on the good around us – what is. Focusing on the good attracts more good to us. Journaling is a powerful transformational tool to connect with our inner selves and Spirit. I keep a gratitude journal to remind myself of my blessings.

Beginning my day in gratitude boosts my energy level and causes my spirit to *soar*. I appreciate my blessings. Viewing the world with optimism, I choose to see the glass as half full rather than half empty. Gratitude helps me see life from a different perspective and paves the way for new opportunity to come into my life. Positive energy fills every fiber of my being.

That for which we are grateful expands and multiplies. Take time daily to sit in gratitude and reflect on that for which you are grateful. Write down the many things in your life that you have been blessed to receive. Keep a daily journal of the things that enrich your life, big or small. Appreciation for life boosts your sense of well-being. When you practice this over time you will come to feel the aliveness in your being.

Gratitude springs positive endorphins into action, changing our attitudes and propelling us to higher, fuller expressions of who we are. As our spirits *soar* we view life from a whole new perspective. Positive expectations, practiced consistently, free our minds to enjoy life better, problem-solve more effectively, explore options, and take effective action to move toward our dreams. They can facilitate healing any aspect of our lives, such as finances, health, and sense of direction.

> As I was writing *Soaring*, there were major fires burning in my area, and we had to evacuate. As I packed I expressed gratitude for my home. I silently affirmed that there was no need to pack heavily because I would be returning. Gratitude and positive expectancy on my part did not stop the fire from burning my home, but it made me feel better in the process as I expressed deep gratitude for the years God had allowed me to live in positive expectancy. One day later we were able to return home unscathed by the fires.

Focusing on the Joy

Letting go of the negatives and looking at the positives are important aspects of *soaring*. To fly easily and comfortably at higher altitudes, it is important to release any weight-bearing attributes such as anger and resentment and replace them with gratitude and positive expectancy. ***Rather than looking at what is wrong with our world, we can look at what is working and focus on what we can do to make it more effective.*** This helps buoy our spirits and brighten our world-view.

To develop an attitude of gratitude, notice the good in your life. Look around you. What is going well in your world? Express joy for what is. For example, I am grateful for the sunshine and the rain. The sun brightens my day and makes me smile. Rain makes beautiful flowers grow. Both bring me joy. I recall when a flight that I was about to embark on was cancelled due to a storm. I am grateful that I was able to learn the information before going to the airport. I am equally grateful that I booked another flight with little ado. Being grateful generates more to be grateful for.

Sometimes life does not go as expected. Issues arise. Challenges occur. Our aim is to look for the positives in the situation. In *The Magic of the Soul*, Patrick J. Harbula says:

> *When we look back on challenging moments, we usually recognize them as moments of intense growth. In retrospect, we may even feel blessed for having gone through them. My suggestion, or really, my*

echo of the ongoing suggestion from your own soul, from all souls, from the collective soul, is to recognize each blessing in the moment.

We can look for the good in each situation. It is there; we simply have to find it and live from that perspective. There is even magic in sadness if one looks hard enough. What is the upside to living in gratitude?

My friend transitioned to another expression of life which we refer to as death. Because I believe that we live in a changeless reality in which life is eternal, I call it a transition to another reality.

When his daughter, Sara, called to inform me, shocked by the suddenness and saddened by the loss of my friend I exclaimed, "No! No!" She, on the other hand, who had every reason to be sad and in disbelief, focused on the beauty. "We had a wonderful evening together with family and a longtime friend. We laughed, had fun, and my father, who had been ill, told each of us what he would say if he were 'checking out.' After a beautiful evening of love and caring, four hours later he made his transition."

Sara was able to see the gift in the situation. Because she was filled with gratitude, she was able to express appreciation for the beautiful transition and the happiness they had shared, and the love with which her father had spent his last day with his family.

I also experienced the same gratitude when my mother of ninety-four years transitioned to a new life. We had a glorious birthday celebration for her during which she expressed gratitude for her life and addressed each of us individually, thanking us for our contributions to her life. That evening she went to the hospital and the next day she quietly slept away to her new reality.

What is significant about each of these situations is that both were grounded in gratitude. Both the persons leaving as well as those who were left behind were filled with love and gratefulness. Living love and gratitude makes life more meaningful and happy. The ability to see the joy in life, whatever is going on, is *soaring*.

Increasing Your Altitude

Look around you. Take a look at what's going on in your world. What makes you happy? What brings you joy? Open your awareness to life. What happened today that pleased you that you perhaps took for granted? Write them down in a gratitude journal and express appreciation for them. Acknowledge the positive and express gratitude for what is going well in your life.

When we express gratitude, the Law of Attraction facilitates more aspects of our lives to work well. Appreciation lifts our spirits and changes fear and doubt into joy and positive expectancy. Practicing gratitude as an ongoing aspect of our lives boosts our energy, changes our attitude, increases our altitude, and empowers us to *soar* with an attitude of gratitude.

You are on a trajectory to *soar*. Lift off!

Applying This *Flight Lesson* in Your Life

1. Keep a gratitude journal in which you write at least five things for which you are grateful each day. Check in with yourself at the end of a week. Are you feeling a deeper appreciation for life?

2. Think of a challenge you face/faced in your life. Reframe it as an opportunity. What can you learn from the experience? What is the gift?

3. Express appreciation to others for small things. Brightening someone else's day will definitely brighten yours.

FLIGHT LESSON SEVEN

Praying To Increase Altitude

Prayer is the sustaining force in my life. I live in constant union with the Source of all life. It is my power and my guide. This morning as I walked in the cool, fresh breeze, I felt the Presence in and around me. As I filled my lungs with the breath of Spirit, the breath of Love, I basked in the joy. Spirit was alive and awake in me. With each breath I breathed in the Divine Essence.

The aim of this *Flight Lesson* is to share with you the influence prayer has in my life and to invite you to explore a prayer practice to enhance your own sense of well-being and achieve your goals. Different spiritual practices have their own different paths to prayer and connection. Whatever that is for you and however you choose to connect with your spiritual essence, it can enhance our lives, our sense of well-being. Deep within my being is Spirit. It is in, around, and through me. I live my life immersed in It, basking in Its glow. As I go within and feel my oneness with Spirit, I *soar*. You can, too.

Thoughts Are Prayers

Even though we may not be aware of it, we are always praying. Our thoughts are prayers. Prayer is an important avenue to reach *soaring altitude.*

> During my dark night of the soul prior to my late husband's transition, I left a successful career to be at home with him. Each morning I walked and talked to God. I did not have a particular formula to evoke the Presence. I simply walked and talked. I would say, "I know that You didn't give me this Ph.D. to stay home, prepare meals, and wash dishes. I know it. The right and perfect opportunity is seeking me."

> Despite my words, I made no inquiries nor sent any resumes concerning employment. I simply affirmed my inner truth that my presence was required at home at that time, and that Spirit would resolve my employment issue. My husband suggested that we go in two directions at once. He would work on getting well and I would work on restarting my career. I could not conceive of taking my heavy heart to appointments. I only did so when I was sought out and when I felt I could sustain a happy face for a short period of time, for my heart was really hurting.

> One day a short position description showed up. To this day I have no idea when and how I received it. It read, "Entrepreneur,

Educator, Business person; Director of Corporate Education" required at a local University. I put the announcement down and did not pick it up again until when en route from a chemotherapy appointment with my husband I noticed the closing date for application. No resumes were being accepted; application on the University's standardized form only was due that day. I began working on the application during the ride home from his treatment. At the end of a long day and a long ride home, I submitted the application minutes before the close of business. I later learned that I was the leading candidate in a long list of candidates, and remained so through the various screenings until I landed the position.

So just what is prayer? Prayer is going within and connecting with Spirit. It is my time to talk with Spirit; not to ask for something, but to acknowledge that there is a Higher Power and to feel Its presence.

Prayer means different things to different people. It is the time we set aside for conscious connection to the Divine. Your experience of the Divine may be an entirely different experience than mine, and not all prayer is tied to a religion. Yoga, tai chi, and other forms of spiritual connection are also routes to connecting to our spiritual essence.

I believe that prayer is an essential element in living in peace and harmony, achieving our dreams easily, and comfortably creating the experience I call *soaring*.

When I pray, I tap in to the Divine Essence. I know the force of the Universe is behind me. The Power and Presence, the Source of all good is supporting me. I let go of worry. I pursue my life unencumbered and inspired. Spirit is everywhere and I am one with It. I live in joy. You, too, can live this joy.

So the question is how does one reach this altered state of awareness through prayer? How does one reach *soaring* altitude? No doubt you have your own approach to prayer, and as I've stated, there is no specific format or a right or wrong way to pray.

There are many routes to connect to our spiritual essence. Prayer that supports our vision, life purpose, passion, and dreams, spoken with faith, conviction, and joyous expectation on a regular basis, and that does not hurt or harm others, moves us toward our dreams. It changes our outlook on life and the way we relate with others. It can change our attitude, our world-view, and our *soaring altitude*.

During my conversations with Spirit I affirm:

1. Spirit is all there is.

2. I am one with Spirit, the Essence of all Life, the Life Force.

3. I declare my intentions, hopes, desires, and vision as already accomplished in my mind and in the mind of Spirit.

4. I express gratitude for the accomplishment of my desired outcome.

5. I release my word to the power of the Universe to accomplish it. I let go and let God.

Ernest Holmes, founder of Religious Science, and Charles Fillmore, founder of the Unity Church, call this form of prayer *affirmative prayer*. In affirmative prayer you recognize and acknowledge Spirit (or whatever you call your Higher Power). You affirm Its presence within you and operating through your affairs. You state with firm conviction and absolute certainty that your desired outcome will manifest in your life.

Express gratitude for the gift already realized in your mind, and release it to Spirit's perfect expression. Positive faith in your desired outcome, spoken with strong belief until you realize it in your own mind, attracts the power of the Universe to support you. Affirmative prayer realizes the power of Spirit expressing in you to heal any condition or situation and manifest your desired outcome.

The difference between this form of praying and *petitionary prayer* is that affirmative prayer is of faith and knowing – knowing that the answer to the prayer is in the prayer. Recall the words of the Master Teacher, Jesus: "As you have believed, it is done unto you" (Mathew 8:13). You do not beg or plead. You have faith and conviction with absolute certainty that your prayer will be answered. You express gratitude for the gift as already given. Spirit is in you and responsive to your thoughts. As you pray you tap in to the mind of Spirit, and through your belief in Spirit, your prayers are realized.

We Are Always Praying

Perhaps you spend time in nature, walking at the beach or watching a beautiful sunset, drinking it in, becoming one with it, enjoying the awe and wonder of it all, allowing the beauty to flow through you. Gratitude wells up in your spirit. Your appreciation may be considered a prayer from your mind to Spirit to spend more time in the Presence.

It is important to remember that prayer is more than the formal time we set aside to go within and connect with Spirit. The thoughts between our prayers are also prayers. In *The Sacred Continuum,* Stephanie Sorensen tells us that the thoughts between the formal times set aside for prayer are just as powerful in creating our experiences:

> *Therefore, if we want to change our lives for good, we must become aware of our thoughts and words as we think and speak them, because the space between prayers is sacred, too. Whether we are acknowledging and directing it or not, the Presence is always present, and the Creative Power within us is always at work turning our thoughts into things and our words into the experiences of our life.*

So what are the implications of the thoughts between our prayers? We are always speaking into the creative realm. As we speak it, we create it. It is important that we monitor our thoughts and speak only what we desire to show up in our lives. We can learn to monitor our thoughts. When we say negative things to ourselves we can learn to reframe them or use words such as "Cancel! Cancel!" to remove the negative thoughts from our awareness. A woman in one of my classes uses the words "Delete! Delete!" By so doing we remind ourselves to release negative messages and let go of doubt and fear. We expect good and only good. In turn, the Universe responds in kind.

Prayers spoken on a regular basis with conviction, love, and gratitude manifest in our lives. Spirit is at the center of our beings and we do not have to go through any spiritual system to unify with this Power. The Power and Presence is in everything, and *we* summon It by our beliefs.

Praying to Increase Your Altitude

I believe prayer works. I also believe that forming a clear picture in our minds of the situation or condition that we want the Universe to resolve manifests results. There has been a multitude of research, with inconsistent findings, on the efficacy of prayer to produce results. Research does show, however, that prayer impacts people's feelings of hopefulness and inner peace, which in turn creates opportunities for positive changes in their experiences and increases their altitude. I invite you to do your own research. As I go within and feel my oneness with Spirit, I *soar*. I invite you to see what a difference it can make in your life.

Applying This *Flight Lesson* in Your Life

1. During the next week, set aside time daily to contemplate your Higher Power and communicate in your mind with your Higher Power.

2. Take into mind your vision. Contemplate what a *soaring* lifestyle means to you. Imagine you are content, happy, your finances are in order, and your relationships are intact. What is required to get you there? What needs to change?

3. What outcome would you like to manifest through the power of prayer?

4. In your mind remember the Power and Presence of Spirit to do all things. State your desired outcome affirmatively. See the goal accomplished in your mind.

5. Express gratitude. Release the desired goal to the Universe and let it go. Continue this practice until the desired change manifests in your life.

FLIGHT LESSON EIGHT

Meditating to Regenerate Your Spirit

Soaring is taking time to let go of the cares of the day; to surrender to the Magnificent Essence within and let go. It is a metaphysical state of mind.

Meditation is an important *soaring* practice as it enables us to rest, relax, and restore our minds; to remember the Divine as well as to access our intuition and listen to our inner voice. Spiritually, meditation is a pathway to our Higher Power. The purpose of meditation is to experience God; to surrender. Meditation is time in the silence to experience the Divine. This consciousness of Spirit empowers us to *soar.*

> I live in the Omnipresence and consciously connect with Spirit daily. Yesterday I chose a walking meditation. My schedule allowed time to either meditate or walk, both activities that take me into Spirit. I chose to combine the two: walk and meditate. I began with prayers of gratitude as I immersed myself in the Magnificence all

around me. I walked mindfully, enjoying each step, filling myself with the beauty of Spirit. I drank in the shapes of the leaves, the flowers, and the bark formations on the trees. Yes, Spirit was everywhere present and in me. I drank from the elixir of all life. I *soared*. I arrived home renewed and refreshed. Thank you, Spirit!

There are many types of and approaches to meditation growing out of different traditions. Perhaps the simplest approach of all is to sit in silence, focusing on your breath to quiet your mind.

Mindfulness meditation, also known as sitting meditation, focuses on helping us to be unconditionally present with whatever is going on in the moment, such as sounds, senses, and feelings. It grows out of the Buddhist thinking that whenever we want something different than what is, we suffer. The aim of this method is to train the mind to be present in the moment and reach a state of inner calm. Movement meditations such as yoga and tai chi combine meditation with movement.

Sound meditations include mantras in which individuals reverently recite a word or phrase known as a mantra as an avenue to move from thinking to calmness. For example, one seeking inner peace can use a mantra such as "peace," "love," or qualities of God to reach a state of inner calm. Kirtan is another form of sound meditation in which one reconnects with the higher self to move inward through musical chants. There are also guided meditations in which a leader uses guided imagery or music to lead others in meditation on wellness, healing, or other qualities they choose to enjoy.

My friend Marsha once said to me, "What is meditation? What does meditation feel like? How will I know when I'm meditating?" Marsha said that she watched her neighbor each morning take a cup of coffee and sit on her patio in deep reflection. She said to herself, "That must be meditation. I want to spend time like her and reach the inner peace she appears to be experiencing." Then one day while Marsha was sitting in her favorite chair, knitting, with the sun beaming on her through the window, she felt a sense of inner peace and calm. "Was I meditating?" Marsha asked.

No doubt each of these women reached a meditative state. The meditation to which I refer is purposely quieting the mind to experience Spirit. When you focus on your breath in the silence, no matter the desired end, it is the breath of Spirit. In *The Joy of Meditation,* Jack Addington writes, "*Meditation is drinking deep from the well of the Spirit.*" The joy of meditation is in the bliss of experiencing union with Spirit.

Psalm 46:10 says, "*Be still and know that I am God.*" Meditation is being still and connecting to your Source. It is a powerful tool in your *Flight Plan* to rest, relax, and regenerate body and spirit. Nourishing your spirit daily empowers you to *soar.*

Choosing Your Method

This *Flight Lesson* encourages you to explore meditation as an option to bring more meaning and purpose to your life. If you have tried meditation and stopped, perhaps another form of meditation better suits your need. Meditation is a personal experience. There are no set rules and there are many different approaches. There are also books, tapes, and instructions and guided meditations online. Explore the various types and choose the approach that best suits you. You may also wish to attend a class or get an instructor to help you meditate.

> I began my meditation practice listening to meditative music and guided meditations to begin and end my day. Initially, listening to music was my practice. I would sit in the silence and allow the music to quiet my mind before I began my prayers. Soon I noticed that I would move from my chair to the floor and begin gentle stretches to the music. This awareness led me to add yoga to my sitting practice, enabling me to simultaneously train my mind and body. Now I sit in the silence allowing my breath to move me inward.

Meditation for me is a period of deep listening. This book grew out of periods of such listening. Each of us is a channel for Spirit. As I listen in the silence I hear Spirit's messages for me, messages I now share with you.

Accessing Your Inner Wisdom

Soaring is a deep awareness of Spirit and a confidence that as spiritual beings our lives are unfolding in perfect right order, and that whatever we desire that does not hurt or harm anyone else is available to us through Divine guidance. In the silence, Spirit informs and guides us. Through meditation we tap in to intuition, our inner knowing, and our higher self. Meditation is the navigational system on our flight. Within each of us is Divine intuition, a part of us that knows the way, a part of us that is creative. Meditation is a way to quiet the mind and access our inner knowing.

> There was a time in my life when I received simultaneous offers to affiliate with two different universities. What should I do? Which was the better offer? I prayed, meditated, and waited for the answer. In meditation, I made the decision and had a successful tenure at the university I chose.

Meditation allows you to tap in to your inner self, to access your inner knowing, the spiritual essence within that empowers you to *soar*. Time in the silence informs you, heals you, and guides you to your truth. Time in the silence gives the seeds of your vision the opportunity to germinate and grow while keeping your flight on course.

Along with its spiritual benefits, meditation eliminates stress and improves your overall sense of well-being. Many people meditate to quiet their mind-chatter and improve physical and mental health. Dr. Herbert Benson, in his landmark research for the book *The Relaxation Response,* discovered many years ago that lowering stress through practices such as meditation boosts the mind and benefits the entire body. His work demystified meditation and corroborated other studies that show that meditation can help reverse heart disease, reduce pain, and support the immune system, facilitating the body's capacity to fight disease.

Contemplating the Sacred

Begin by finding a quiet, comfortable place, sitting with your palms in your lap facing upward. Close your eyes and focus on your breathing, finding a slow, rhythmic pattern. Take long, slow breaths to relax your body and slow your mind. Continue deep, rhythmic breathing until you reach a sense of inner peace and calm. As thoughts pass through your mind, gently allow them to come and go, focusing on your breath. Simply breathe and allow calmness to gradually flow over you, and seek to realize a state of inner peace. Meditation is a time to contemplate the Sacred. This may not be easy initially. However, the mind can be trained. With practice, your experience of meditation can deepen. Begin with five minutes and gradually increase the time. Over time your practice can increase.

Mantra Meditation

Choose a word that has meaning or a quality that you would like to see in your life. Some typical words are *love*; *peace*; *shanti*, the Hindu word for peace; and *Om*, the word for Universal Love. Choose a mantra to repeat. Close your eyes and focus on your breathing, finding a slow, rhythmic pattern. Take long, slow breaths to relax your body and slow your mind as you repeat your mantra. Continue deep, rhythmic breathing until in the quiet you reach a sense of inner calm. As thoughts pass through your mind, gently allow them to come and go, focusing on your mantra. Simply breathe, allow calmness to gradually flow over you, and seek to realize the Presence.

Moving to *Soaring* Altitude

As you explore and incorporate these *Flight Lessons* in your life you may find your attitude and approach to life changing. Time spent in quietness nourishes your spirit and provides guidance through intuition. Connecting with the Divine in prayer changes the way you look at things, and the circumstances in your life change. When you focus on the positives in your life you find your positive experiences expanding. That which you focus on grows. The Law of Attraction brings more positive experiences into your life as you practice being positive. As you express gratitude for the good in your life, your outlook on life changes. Your spirit moves even higher in consciousness. You have reached *soaring* altitude.

Applying This *Flight Lesson* in Your Life

1. What is your goal in meditation?

   - To heighten spiritual awareness?

   - Resolve a health issue?

   - Reduce stress?

   - Access your intuition?

   - Something else?

2. Explore the various types of meditation and choose a method that best suits you.

3. Practice at least five minutes daily to regenerate your spirit, and gradually increase the time until you are able to find a comfortable level of meditation for you.

4. As issues arise in your life, spend time in meditation asking questions and listening. For example, you might silently ask, "What is the next step for me?" Your inner wisdom will inform you.

Forgiving to Forget

Is an old hurt, anger, or resentment holding you back and blocking your spirit? Do you have old wounds to heal? Sometimes forgiving others for hurting us is one of the most difficult things to do. Yet most of us have been hurt by the behavior or words of others at one time or another in our lives. Harboring resentment bogs us down and interferes with the flow of life. This heaviness interferes with our ability to *soar* inspired and unencumbered. Unresolved hurts result in additional pain and suffering. Forgiveness is a *soaring* practice that releases us from the past, opens our hearts, and allows our love to flow more freely. Forgiveness improves physical, emotional, and spiritual health, and frees us to *soar*.

Healing Old Hurts

A young manager seeking a marriage counselor to resolve issues prior to a new marriage shared with me that she had been raped at gunpoint as a student. Although she received counseling at the time, and years had gone by, her pain was still just below the surface. Discussing her anger and feelings of powerlessness at the time she said, "Some days I go looking for a fight." Imagine carrying that burden daily while trying to live your life! Sessions with her therapist helped her resolve the anger and move on to having a successful marriage.

When we hold on to anger and resentment, it saps our energy, blocking our path to resolution. We are the ones to experience the pain while the other person may not even be aware of our discomfort. Dr. Fred Luskin, in his book *Forgive for Good,* calls this "renting space in our consciousness." When we allow an event or circumstance to rent space in our consciousness or remain heavy in our heart, we tend to hold on to the story using valuable energy in the constant retelling of our injustice. Our sense of right and wrong has been offended and our ego wants redress. Seeking relief, we go around and around on the merry-go-round of life, seeking support from those who will listen while we stay mired in the story. This desire for retribution does nothing to the person who hurt us; it hurts only us. Ann Landers is credited with saying, *"Hate is like an acid. It damages the vessel in which it is stored, and destroys the vessel on which it is poured."*

Forgiveness frees you to move on with your life, allowing you to be the expression of Spirit you came here to be. Forgiveness lets you take responsibility for how you feel and look for a pathway to your healing. When Nelson Mandela walked out of prison he said he left all the hatred behind. Otherwise he would have been a prisoner for the rest of his life.

Jim, a tall, handsome, muscular young man, sat slouched in his chair, the pain of depression clearly showing on his face. He looked down as he talked, barely able to make eye contact with me. Seething with anger he described his injustice: a wrongful stop, an incarceration, and a successful career interrupted. He wanted only revenge, had engaged attorneys to "get back his life," and wanted to hear nothing of freeing up his energy to move on. The responsible parties needed to pay! Jim got in touch with the pain beneath his anger and found positive ways to expend his energy, empowering himself. He returned to school, focused on physical fitness, and over time resumed his career.

Clearing the Circuits

The first step in forgiveness is to acknowledge our pain and hurt.

I have come to experience life as all God and all good, so little offends me. Typically I seek not to judge, but to accept others as they are. I forgive as events occur with an attitude of "and so it is: that part of life that just is."

When I do feel hurt, I journal my feelings, including any anger I may feel. I ask myself, "What is this about? Why do I feel hurt?" Typically the person has violated my expectation or some long-held rule that I regard as being right or wrong. Yes, you guessed it, my ego is involved. During journaling, I see the person as love, and lay out action steps for letting the issue go or formulate a win-win strategy to resolve the situation. I pray and meditate on forgiveness until the matter no longer occupies a major spot in my thinking. Mentally affirming my forgiveness over time usually resolves the sting of the hurt.

If I feel the situation merits further attention, I go through a period of self-reflection and problem-solving, and take appropriate action that may include sharing and resolving the issue with the other person. For example, at one time in my life I did not receive what I felt was a much-deserved promotion. I let it go initially, yet would wake up in the middle of the night and ask why I hadn't received it. I decided to explore the issue further, and I, too, ended up with a promotion based on my own merit.

Forgiveness is coming to peace with a situation. Sometimes we are not able to easily resolve the situation because the hurt is longstanding or the pain is so deep that deeper work is needed. If so, you may consider getting help from a professional.

In the book *Radical Forgiveness*, Colin Tipping shares a process to help us let go of anger and blame, find peace, and move to a place of gratitude. Tipping suggests:

1. Tell and own your story in the first person, identifying the pain you experience. For example, "I feel hurt when my daughter spends holidays with her in-laws rather than spending time with me." This is more effective than thinking, "My daughter's constant snubbing of me on holidays ticks me off!"

2. Feel the pain of the situation by acknowledging the hurt you feel.

3. Understand the false belief that is keeping you entrapped in the victim role and make a decision to stop giving power to the other person. The false belief is that someone else has power to hurt you. For example, your happiness during holidays does not depend on seeing your daughter and grandchildren on the actual holiday.

4. Reframe the story to take back your power and resolve the conflict. For example, arranging another day mutually agreeable to both of you allows you to see the children, feel the joy, and retain a sense of your own power.

5. Finally, look for the gift in the situation. What benefit did you learn from this entire experience? Perhaps seeing the children on another day during the holidays garnered two gifts: seeing the children and family peace. Express gratitude for your gift.

Tipping's approach is considered radical because it not only asks us to forgive the other person, it also asks us to be grateful for the learning the experience affords us. In the situation discussed above one could be grateful for the opportunity to handle the situation in a way that allows one to enjoy the family during the holiday in a spirit of love, free of hurt.

> As a young professional, I was led to expect a promotion. My manager enthusiastically recommended me for the promotion, anxious to display this young, new talent, only to return from a departmental meeting to tell me that I would have to "wait my turn." Although disappointed, rather than being angry and resentful I applied for graduate school, choosing to be grateful for the gift in the situation. I wasn't stuck in the bureaucracy. My spirit was free to *soar* to different experiences and higher heights.

Many people have chosen forgiveness and gratitude in lieu of pain and suffering after life-changing events. Examples are veterans returning from war, survivors of 9/11, and most recently the Boston Marathon bombing survivors. Perhaps one of the more moving stories of forgiveness arising out of catastrophe is the story of Immaculee Ilibagiza, author of *Left to Tell*. Immaculee's family was slaughtered in the Rwandan war, and the murderers looked for her while she huddled silently for ninety-one days in the bathroom of her pastor's home with seven other women, all of them full of terror. During this period Immaculee prayed and formed a profound relationship with God through which she found love and forgiveness. Through this strong bond Immaculee was able to seek out and forgive her family's killers.

In *Forgive for Good*, Dr. Fred Luskin defines forgiveness as "*the feeling of peace that emerges as you take hurt less personally, take responsibility for how you feel, and become a hero instead of a victim in the story you tell.*" You become a hero by assuming responsibility for your feelings and using your personal power to overcome hurt rather than remaining a victim. His research demonstrates that forgiveness results in improved mental and physical health.

We can take responsibility for how we feel, focus on the good in our lives, and change our thinking from painful thoughts to ones of gratitude, beauty, forgiveness, and love. We can also use deep breathing and meditation to let go of pain and focus on the present.

Regaining Your Power

Life doesn't always go according to our rules. Some life events hurt and disappoint us. Forgiveness is letting go of the pain and disappointment when life appears to wrong us. As we gain altitude in our progression to *soaring*, we learn to let go of the victim mentality without anger or negative emotions.

You are in charge of your own life. You no longer occupy your thinking with someone else who may or may not know about or understand your pain. Letting go means you are independent and free to move on with your life. Use your energy to set new goals. During the healing process, treat yourself with love and compassion. Spend time in nature, take long walks, or get a massage. Take time to nurture your mind, body, and spirit. The next *Flight Lesson* shares more information regarding how to nurture yourself.

Increasing Your Altitude

Meanwhile, stop telling the story. Release it, let it go, and tell a new story. Why not tell how you overcame this obstacle and regained a sense of your own power?

Look for the silver lining. What is the growth opportunity for you? What did you learn from this experience? Unleash your own power and turn this situation into an opportunity. Create joy out of this pain and reward yourself for each level of altitude you gain.

As you do so, send a blessing to the person who offended you. Use your energy to bring peace and joy to your own life. Use the meditation *soaring* practices learned in *Flight Lesson Seven* to rest and restore your inner peace. Take responsibility for your own happiness and move to higher altitude with grace and gratitude. Forgiveness frees you to *soar.*

Applying This *Flight Lesson* in Your Life

1. Identify a situation in your life in which you need to forgive yourself or someone else.

2. Write a letter to the person who aggrieved you. Identify the offense and express your hurt.

3. What is the belief that causes you to hold on to your story? How can you remove yourself from the role of victim in this situation? Picture yourself not as a recipient of abuse, but as one who can use your power to take charge of your life and move on.

4. Look for the silver lining. What is the gift for you in the situation? How can you grow from this experience?

5. Make an Action Plan. What action steps can you take to move forward in your life?

My Forgiveness Action Plan

Goal:

What	How	Who	When
1.			
2.			
3.			
4.			
5.			

Goal:

What	How	Who	When
1.			
2.			
3.			
4.			
5.			

FLIGHT LESSON TEN

Encountering Turbulence

Although we have learned *Flight Lessons* for flying smoothly in previous chapters, sometimes in handling the vicissitudes of life we encounter turbulence. Sometimes we seek change; at other times our world begins to move around us. A crisis occurs. Accidents happen. We find ourselves in the throes of change.

> I was *soaring*, enjoying the view from the top. There were no clouds in the sky. What a beautiful world! I was in love with my husband, my career, and my life. I literally felt on top of the world. I came home from a trip, greeted my husband who looked as healthy and handsome as ever. He informed me that he had been diagnosed with asthma. We both questioned this sudden onset and a comprehensive examination revealed stage four lung cancer. My life flipped upside down.
>
> That same morning we had a final review with the contractor for the new home we were planning. The news put the contract

and my whole life on hold. One phase of my world stood still while the rest of my world changed quickly and dramatically. Although it was not clear to me then, this was the journey for which Spirit was preparing me – a long, sometimes dark journey was awaiting me.

At the time my spiritual consciousness was new and fluid. I had been so busy enjoying life that I had devoted little time to nurturing a spiritual practice. Although I believed in positive thinking, affirmations, and visualization, I was not actively practicing them. To allay my fears during the diagnostic process, I envisioned us growing old together. I was quite unprepared for the doctors' findings. I turned to Spirit. The twenty-third Psalm became my ongoing prayer and affirmation.

The Lord is my shepherd; I shall not want.
He maketh me to lie down in
green pastures: he leadeth me
beside the still waters.
He restoreth my soul: he leadeth
me in the paths of righteousness
for his name's sake.
Yea, though I walk through the valley
of the shadow of death, I will fear no
evil: for thou art with me; thy rod
and thy staff they comfort me.
Thou preparest a table before me in the
presence of mine enemies: thou anointest
my head with oil; my cup runneth over.

*Surely goodness and mercy shall follow
me all the days of my life: and I will
dwell in the house of the LORD forever.*

I lived in this consciousness. I was grateful for each day I had with my husband after the diagnosis. I chose to really savor and experience loving this wonderful man. We lived a beautiful year in love and gratitude. I was truly grateful each day and very much appreciated his verbal expressions of gratitude to Spirit "for one more day in this beautiful world" as he walked in our garden. One evening his breathing became labored and he peacefully transitioned.

When he left, I continued to feel gratitude for our life together, his peaceful transition, and the support of loved ones and friends. My gratitude list goes on and on. Initially I fell from the top of the world to a deep valley. Spirit became my constant guide. Prayer, love, and gratitude became my way. I made a decision to live each day in positive expectancy. In my heart I knew that although the glass appeared to be half empty, it was brimming over with blessings. I lived in gratitude even as I grieved, affirming that there was a rainbow at the end of the darkness. Each day I continued to walk toward the light with Spirit as my guide. In the process I learned to *soar.*

Dealing with Change

When there is turbulence in our lives it is a critical time to implement the *soaring* practices learned in the *Flight Lessons* in *Soaring*. It is the time to know God's perfection is right where we are: in the situation, in every cell, in every fiber of our being. It is the time to turn away from circumstances, have faith, and embrace our wholeness. It is the time to remember the impact that positive thoughts have on our situation. Send the message into the Universe that only peace and wholeness exist in every atom of our being.

Affirm this message in your prayers, meditation, notes to yourself on your mirror and other places around the house. Most of all, affirm it in your heart. Your immune system at the very structure of your being has the capacity to hear your message and respond accordingly. Meditation and prayer can facilitate healing in body, mind, and spirit. Here are some examples of individuals who used spiritual practices to support them during turbulence in their lives:

> Kari was at the height of her career when one morning in the shower the unthinkable happened: she found a lump in her breast that had not been there the day before. It turned out to be an aggressive form of breast cancer that had only a 25 percent survival rate. Kari immediately sought medical help and turned to prayer, as she knew this would be the truth to her survival as she began a yearlong battle for her life.

She spent her days in gratitude, seizing each moment to find joy wherever she could: walking daily with her husband, meditating, praying, and communicating with friends via her wellness website. After a year of treatment Kari was given the all-clear by her doctors. She is an inspiration to others, and has become a spokesperson for cancer recovery for her doctor, hospital, and community.

Dahlia was on disability from her job for three years when she decided to attend graduate school while looking for a new opportunity that would be less stressful.

Finding difficulty in locating a position on her level, out of funds, mortgage in arrears, she chose to take a position working as a mental health professional in a state mental health facility, something she had never done before. "God has opened this door. I'm going to walk through it," she said. Dahlia has since been promoted several levels to unit director with responsibility for all other allied health professionals. She credited her spiritual practice, faith, and prayer for sustaining her through this trying time.

Soaring practices can provide the confidence sometimes needed to move through difficult times. Pat's mom made a peaceful transition after living a long and beautiful life of love and meaning, and although Pat was married, her mom had been her major support system. Though Pat had brothers, she had grown up as an only child, and she and her mother were very close. Within two years, two of Pat's brothers also transitioned. With the help of grief counseling, Pat recovered. Now her employer is in the process of relocating their business to another state. Although not ready for another major upheaval, Pat's world has begun to change. She needs an anchor to move through what appears to be another life challenge. It is her belief that along with the support of friends and *soaring* practices of prayer, faith, and time in the silence, she can navigate the storm.

Sometimes we are able to proactively manage change. At other times our world appears to move around us without warning and we are required to adapt to unexpected circumstances. How do we build resilience and the ability to adapt to change?

The Power of Choice

We have choices, and those choices create our lives. We may not have the power to choose the events in our lives; we can choose our reactions to them. The choices we make shape our reality. Challenges provide us opportunities to grow.

During times of turbulence is when we remember to have faith and know that Spirit is in every situation. Have faith in the Power and Presence that created you; that is as close to you as the next breath. Have faith that this power is leading you to a positive resolution. Through your belief in a positive outcome you can resolve any challenge.

Flying on the Wings of Faith

During my husband's transition I was buoyed by faith. Sometimes while encountering turbulence we have to rest in the everlasting arms of Spirit and allow our faith to keep us airborne. Faith is the conviction that all is well – the awareness of a reality that you do not see but feel in your heart. It is trust and belief in the realization of your vision, your purpose, and the goodness of life. It is trust and belief in a positive resolution of your challenge.

Faith is belief in Spirit, the Universal Presence that is always working in our lives. Faith that our thoughts create our reality empowers us to handle the challenges in our lives and to view them as opportunities for growth. Each encounter is an opportunity, not a challenge.

> *Faith is the substance of things hoped for,*
> *the evidence of things unseen.*
> *—Hebrews 11:1*

This Biblical wisdom guides us during turbulent times. Belief in your vision, your purpose, and your dream is positive energy, whether in your mind or in concrete form that you can touch, feel, or see. Your thoughts change energy into form. Changing thoughts into form requires faith. Albert Einstein proved that matter and energy are interchangeable. Water is still water no matter in what form it appears – vapor, ice, or liquid. Faith can change the invisible to the visible, your dreams into reality, and your crises into stability.

When life seems difficult it is essential to hold the conviction that all is well and that all will be well. Spirit in you, as you, knows the way, and will support you in your journey as you believe. Belief, acceptance, and trust in this Power facilitate *soaring* during turbulence.

Let Go and Let God

Some of us have a relaxed and laid-back approach to life. Others feel it important to take action and make things happen. There are times to be proactive, and others when it is important to stop struggling with your wants and your fears and trust the Power that created you. Release all attachment to the way you think things should be and *know* that Spirit is supporting you in the resolution of your issue. Let go of all demands. Let go of would've, could've, should've, and surrender to what is. Surrendering is a powerful spiritual practice.

Surrendering is moving away from an approach to life in which we *make* things happen to one in which we *trust* and *allow* things to happen just as they are – we offer no resistance to life. When we surrender we have faith in the creative flow of life. Surrendering is releasing attachments and expectations. It is releasing the need to have something occur in a specific way, at a particular time. We have faith that Spirit is all there is. Through our faith and belief in Spirit we are able to solve any problem.

Practicing Present-Time Awareness

When you want something other than what is, you experience discontentment. When you let go of longing for something other than what is, you practice *present-time awareness* (also known as *mindfulness*). All that really matters is what is going on in the moment. The past is gone, the future is uncertain. You may not have control over what is going on in the moment; you do control your reaction to it. Have faith and trust.

Look for the gift in each situation – the joy as well as the pain. Relax, breathe deeply, and bring peace to the situation during daily meditation. Rather than longing for something other than what is, now is the time to trust life; trust a Power for Good in the Universe is working for you, here and now.

> Sally has a bipolar disorder and undergoes electric shock treatments. She reached out to her spiritual community and built a support network. She attends classes that teach a positive, spiritual approach to living and has created a support system to help her through this period in her life. She is optimistic and happy. A former teacher, now on disability benefits, she envisions a plan for her life in this phase of her journey that includes a new business that uses her skills and helps others. Sally still has her ups and downs, but she relies on prayer,

meditation, and her spiritual community to support her during times of turbulence.

She writes, "*I am aware that the one constant element that has been with me has been my resiliency to overcome the odds that this disease has stacked against me. I have a positive outlook. I have worked to create a good life. I am confident that I will embark on a new career path helping to reduce the stigma coupled with my diagnosis. I am a survivor and ready to follow the road to recovery one day at a time. I attribute my well-being as a gift of a loving God who has been my rock of faith. This personal relationship has facilitated my recovery.*"

Finding Peace in the Moment

Being able to feel my connection to Spirit is my anchor in a storm. When suddenly I found myself alone, I learned to simply sit in the silence and breathe. Take some deep, healing breaths to bring you into spiritual alignment with your center. Relax into knowing that "God is all there is," or choose a positive affirmation to remind you of your desired outcome. I often repeat, "God and I are one," to remind myself that Spirit is as close as my next breath.

When you heal sufficiently from a traumatic event, ask yourself, "What is there to learn from this crisis? What is the gift life has to offer me in this situation? How will I make lemonade out of lemons? How will I grow from the experience?" Remember that though we do not have complete control over the external forces that show up in our lives, we do control our reactions to them.

Soaring is finding peace in the moment. Focus on your breath to practice present-time awareness. Close your eyes, take a deep breath, filling your abdomen for three counts, holding your breath for three counts, and then releasing for three counts. Continue this breathing until you find yourself at peace. Your breath creates space between your thoughts to relax and center yourself.

Who Can Help?

When encountering turbulence it is important to ask yourself who can help. In addition to your own resources and *soaring* practices learned from your *Flight Lessons*, what else is needed? Who or what can ameliorate the situation, ask the right question, or point you in the right direction? Build and use your personal support system for assistance, and when necessary, seek the help of professionals.

> When I was dealing with the grief of my husband's transition, friends suggested grief counseling. Grief counseling? Me? Matti, the strong one, was always in charge. Then one day as I prepared to leave my home for the day, I suddenly sat down and began crying. The grieving little girl inside me who had been dragged along with a happy face while crying and screaming internally refused to go further without attention. I did not want to relive

the pain with a grief therapist. I checked into my favorite health retreat for rest and recuperation and prayed for direction. After praying, I went to the dining room where I met my friend, a psychologist and hypnotherapist, whom I had not seen in a while. My prayer was answered in less than five minutes. I had a hypnotherapy session with him the next day during which I cried and talked to my husband for an hour and a half. When I next went to the dining room a guest remarked, "What happened to you today? You are so much brighter and lighter." Take your situation in prayer and meditation and ask for guidance. Spirit will guide you.

Applying This *Flight Lesson* in Your Life

1. When encountering a crisis, use the *soaring* practices from all the previous lessons.

2. Pray daily to realize the presence of Spirit in the situation. Think of what you would like to resolve or change. State it positively in your mind as an accomplished fact and express gratitude. Release any fear, worry, and doubt. Let go and let God.

3. Write affirmations to state the resolutions you desire.

4. Visualize what you desire as already accomplished in your mind.

5. Ask yourself who can help – family, friends, professionals – and go to them.

6. Notice positive changes and express gratitude.

Nurturing Mind, Body, and Spirit

Live your joy! Love yourself! Take care of the most important person in your life – *you!* Personal nurturing is rejuvenating mind, body, and spirit. What is that for you? What makes your spirit *soar*?

> I find that walking along the beach immediately lifts my energy and aligns me with Spirit. Getting into nature is food for my soul. My day begins with a morning walk during which I bask in the Presence, followed by prayer, meditation, and spiritual reading to nourish my being. I have a dynamic schedule. Time at the beach in the Omnipresence is joy for my soul. In the Omnipresence, I drink from the sweet elixir of all life. My spirit *soars*!

Self-care and nurturing are important practices in living empowered and joyful. Mind, body, and spirit work together to create our mental, physical, and spiritual state of well-being. This *Flight Lesson* recognizes the mind/body/spirit connection and the importance of giving attention to all three for our overall wellness, inner peace, and happiness.

Often we function with an overload of data, information, schedules, places to go, and things to do. Many of us live in the fast lane. Burnout is a major obstacle for high-energy high-achievers. High energy and high demands interact with each other to create opportunities for healing. Self-care is a *Flight Lesson* that I had to repeatedly learn. Having mastered the art of creating opportunities for healing, I recognize the importance of creating a long-term strategy to nurture my physical, mental, and spiritual well-being. Self-care is essential for living an empowered lifestyle. To win you have to be in the game. Remember the airline attendant's instruction: Put your own life mask on first.

What does self-care look like to you? How do you take care of yourself? What awakens you? What energizes you? For some of us it's time in nature, walking in a park, walking in the rain or fog. For me, walking on a foggy, misty day takes me within myself, generating mystical feelings. I see more clearly when the fog has gone, both figuratively and realistically.

Time in nature connects me with Spirit and regenerates my soul. Find a way to ground yourself by connecting with the earth in some way. For example, place your bare feet on the ground and allow the rhythm of the earth to pour into you. Sometimes during my walks I stop to focus on the beauty of a tree. I touch it, push or lean against it, and feel the stability and sturdiness of Spirit. I immerse myself in the beauty of plants or flowers.

Let's find joy in the weather. Enjoy the beauty of snow, rain, sunshine, stars, and natural light. Each activity immerses us in Oneness, our essential being-ness. We are alive! We are awake! We are living Spirit from moment to moment. We are appreciating life. We are in joy. Finding the joy in each moment empowers us to *soar*.

Nurturing You

Too often life is a balancing act (doing versus being), juggling things we think we should be doing instead of being in the flow of life. *Doing* focuses on outer activity. *Being* is inner-directed; it calms and nurtures. Excessive focus on doing rather than nurturing being can create burnout.

> Kim, the director of a pharmaceutical company, received an international assignment and had two months to plan the trip, make arrangements for her family, acculturate to a new country where she did not speak the language, and facilitate change in the organization's culture. Once there she realized that she was suffering from burnout, and used the experience to both complete the assignment and heal herself through quiet periods of meditation during the time away from the hustle and bustle of her regular schedule back at home. Kim sent me this note:
>
> *Always multitasking, I thought I felt alive by taking care of family, loving God,*

giving back to my community, and being successful professionally. I'd begun to sense I needed to do more. Something was gnawing at me, but I didn't know what. My international assignment was what I thought was this calling. I was thirty days into my assignment, away from my usual routine, when I had a spiritual awakening. I was making the fifteen-minute daily walk to work when suddenly my surroundings came alive. I could see the beauty in the trees, the lake, and see the birds flying. That evening when I returned home I couldn't wait to share my revelation with you. Our conversation helped me understand that everything I'd been doing, professional success, supporting family and friends, was just doing. I was on autopilot... through our discussion I came to the realization that I was in burnout. What a revelation!

As the fog lifted, I began to focus on me. Who am I? What makes me happy? What are my goals for the future? Through our conversations you helped me visualize what I wanted my professional and personal life to feel like. Once I began to visualize my joy and happiness I began to pray, meditate, and speak it into existence. Soon that visualization began to manifest in my personal and professional life. I have received the promotion that I envisioned, resulting in more physical and spiritual joy. I am now in a situation where I have the freedom to escape to the beach, enjoy nature, spend quality time with my family, and nurture my spirit. These are the things that bring me joy! Thanks to your encouragement, I now know the signs and can tell when I begin to slip back into doing. What can I say... it's my nature! However, I understand and know when I begin to drift back into doing and not being. I catch myself and correct quickly by taking time to engage my spirit and reconnect to nature until my feelings of joy leap up in me again. I've learned to just say NO, take frequent trips to the beach, and fill my spirit with joy and happiness along with the hard work.

Elaine represents another example of one living a life of balance and self-care. She is raising her grandson, participates in his sports activities, and carpools. She volunteers at his school and at the local hospital several days a week, plus co-chairs committees at her church. Yet she takes time to play in her garden and find joy in providing support and love to her family. Volunteer activities are sacred service for her. It is giving and receiving love, thereby a deep source of self-nurturing.

Pauline, a college professor, nurtures her grandchildren, visits her ninety-five-year-old aunt in an assisted living facility daily, and recently received a three-day notice to begin a strategic planning assignment in Dubai. To keep in balance she walks every morning, has a spiritual practice, and takes a positive approach to living. Her motto is "I have to 'do me.'"

"Doing me" is taking time to focus on activities that enliven your spirit and promote your sense of well-being. If possible, participate in a network of friends who understand the importance of "Doing me." Hard-working high-achievers recognize that well-being is no longer about amassing more stuff; it is about embracing a passion for life that includes giving, loving, and doing their fair share to make this world a better place. My friend Pauline and her cousin are great examples. They personally cook and serve two hundred meals to the homeless one Sunday a month as a part of their church's sacred service program, feeding their own well-being in the process.

Releasing Old Habits

Perhaps your world is great. You are at the top of your game. Life is going well and you are happy. You feel that it's time to move to a new experience. You are skilled and have a sense of your own power. Yet you want more. You simply have to change your course to the next level. Set your intention and move in the direction of your dreams. Life will support you. At least that's the way it's always happened for me.

I have been writing this book in my mind for years. It was finally time to write it.

How to do it with a full schedule was the big question. Of course some things had to change, but what? I made a schedule. Clients to see, classes to teach, talks to write, and don't forget those unexpected interruptions. I turned to doing what I had always done, attempting to power my way through, work a little longer, work a little harder. Sometimes it is necessary to release old habits and let go of what no longer serves you if you want to move ahead in your life.

When I was a child and my mother gave me an errand to do, I ran. I remember her words well: "Walk, don't run." That is a lesson my mother taught me, though I never really learned it. My internal message to myself was "Get it done! Get it done fast! Get it done right!" Yes, that was my modus operandi. Falling back into that old habit when I began to write *Soaring* landed me in the emergency room with neck spasms. Pushing and attempting to work faster, harder, powering my way through, had failed again. Working harder and longer did not accomplish the goal and it never will. Shortening the prayer and meditation part of my day does not provide additional time; it saps my energy. Time in the silence revitalizes and regenerates me.

When we realize that there is a Power for Good in the Universe and that we can trust the Power for Good that created us, we stop struggling to have it all, to do it all, and relax into knowing that whatever the unplanned demand on our time might be, it is okay. Life is unfolding in perfect, right order. The timing is just as it should be. We release old habits and practice living in the now.

Pursuing multiple goals is a balancing act. Whether you are at the top of your vocation; starting your career; juggling school, work and a household; or working in the international arena, nurturing your mind, body, and spirit is essential for optimum living.

Mind, body, and spirit are one interrelated system. Change in any one part impacts the others. Your physical body is the temple that houses all the systems. Nurturing each part of this intricately related system keeps all the other parts functioning optimally.

Nurturing Your Mind

Your mind is the major driver to keep the other systems functioning well. Nurturing your mind is a key component of self-care. Optimism and positive thinking lay the foundation for nurturing our minds. Pay attention to what you are thinking and monitor your thoughts. Choose thoughts that are empowering and lift your spirits.

Your thoughts create your life. Someone once said, "Look at how you are living; it will tell you what you are thinking." Nurturing your mind is focusing on your life's purpose, living in the moment, and letting go of negative thinking and replacing it with positive thoughts that give you optimism and hope.

Living Mindfully

Present-time awareness is focusing on what is. It is actually paying attention to what you are doing as you move through the day. "Practicing the present" is surrendering to and accepting what is going on in the moment without judging or evaluating – it simply is. Eckhart Tolle refers to this as "practicing the now." Practicing the now is internal awareness of your connection to Spirit from moment to moment. It is alertness to Spirit deep within you, awareness of the aliveness within you, and appreciating from where it comes. It is learning to practice stillness as you move about in daily life.

Have you ever tried to perform an activity and really be present during the activity? Eckhart Tolle suggests paying attention as you perform routine activities such as washing your hands. While washing your hands, feel the sensation of the water as it ripples across your hands and be with the feeling. This concentration is called mindfulness.

Paying attention to the feel of your feet in each step you take as you walk is practicing mindfulness. Take a deep breath, hold, and slowly release it. As you breathe, pay attention to the feel of your breath as it enters your nostrils and moves into your airways, the tension you feel while holding it, and the relief from releasing it. These are ways to stay in the moment and alleviate compulsive thinking generated by stress and worry.

Present-time awareness reduces stress and changes it into gratitude and appreciation. Dr. Jon Kabat-Zinn refers to this as "living mindfully." Living mindfully does not necessarily change the situation; it changes our perceptions about the situation, often lifting our spirits. Check in with yourself during the day. Pay attention to where you are. Take a deep breath and bring mindfulness to your activity. Mindful living reduces stress, anxiety, and pain, and facilitates enjoying life. It empowers you to *soar.*

In his book *Full Catastrophe Living*, Dr. Kabat-Zinn describes the Mindful Stress Reduction and Relaxation Program at the University of Massachusetts Medical School, in which individuals learned to not only manage their health issues and stressors, but to appreciate life more fully through practicing mindful stress reduction. Individuals participated in an intense eight-week program in which they learned to meditate daily and practice present-time awareness. Dr. Kabat-Zinn suggests practicing mindfulness in day-to-day living as a way to reduce stress and enjoy life more fully.

Being Here Now

Present-time awareness is a wonderful way to nurture mind, body, and spirit and reduce stress. Removing future orientation and releasing worry about the past frees us to be in the moment – to enjoy what is. I had a yoga instructor who periodically asked, "What time is it?" to bring our awareness to the present moment. Our response was, "Now!" He would then ask, "Where are you?" We would respond, "Here!"

Present-time awareness allows us to be in the moment, whatever is going on, be it joy or pain. During joyful moments, being present allows us to really appreciate the moment. Mindful practice can also reduce the pain of loss or illness by training us to accept rather than resist a situation. Reducing resistance to pain or loss reduces stress and allows us to cope more effectively with a situation. Accepting the present empowers us to see the beauty, the lesson to be learned, and transcend the pain. It is an important *soaring* practice for nurturing the mind and practicing self-care.

Nurturing Your Body

It has long been established that a healthy diet, rest, and exercise are key to keeping your system functioning. Each of us is unique. Although there are basic guidelines, what constitutes an appropriate diet and sufficient rest differs for each of us. It is important to find your own balance – what works for your optimum sense of well-being.

Along with a healthy diet, periodic detoxification and deep cleansing of the body support a healthy physical system. In support of my personal care I periodically attend an optimum health program aimed toward mind, body, and spiritual rejuvenation. The program provides a healthy, raw diet of organic foods and juices as well as various adjunct modalities such as toning, stretching, and deep-breathing classes to nourish mind, body, and spirit. I leave feeling regenerated and invigorated.

Let's not forget those mandatory annual physical check-ups. If there is something amiss in your physical system, early diagnosis and treatment are important to keep your body temple in prime condition.

Along with a healthy diet, the body requires touch to flourish and grow. Hugs, massages, and physical interaction are vital to overall physical well-being. Research on institutionalized babies conducted by Drs. Renee Spitz and John Bowlby during WWII demonstrated that although fed and changed, without tactile stimulation and sensation, babies did not thrive. Daniel Goleman, in a *New York Times* article published on February 2nd, 1988, called "The Experience of Touch; Research Points to a Critical Role," indicated that being touched has direct and profound effects on growth of the mind and body. Touch nourishes the spirit as well as the physical body. "*Reach out and touch somebody's hand, make this world a better place if you can,*" as sung by Diana Ross in her debut solo album in 1970, simply emphasizes my point. Please don't forget to take care of your own physical well-being. Massage and bodywork not only nourish the physical body, they reduce stress and nourish the spirit as well.

Nurturing Your Spirit

Nurturing your spirit is finding inner peace and harmony. It is recognizing the Divine Presence within and connecting with Spirit through prayer and meditation. In previous *Flight Lessons* we discussed the value of prayer and meditation to feed the soul. Both are basic to living happily and empowered. Grounding yourself in love of self and each other also awakens your inner spirit through joy and connection with family and friends.

You can also nurture yourself in activities that calm and invite introspection, such as reading. Escaping into humor, comedy, and fun activities such as movies, theater, the arts, and time with family and friends also regenerates the spirit.

Finding calm in the middle of the storm is essential. Listen to yourself. Are you exhausted? Running on fumes? Perhaps it is time to look at how much time you are spending performing activities versus truly being in the moment and living life. Look for ways to balance the doing with quiet, reflective, or energizing time to renew your spirit.

Your spirit will inform you of the need for more balance. Check in with yourself. How do you spend your time? Where do you fit on the "Doing versus Being Scale" below?

Being 1 2 3 4 5 6 7 8 9 10 Doing

If you rate yourself higher than six, look to see what needs to change. Where can you reduce the doing and add more quiet, reflective time? Many times I check in with myself and realign my activities to reduce the doing and focus on being – being quiet, being at peace, being in Spirit, being in the moment, being one with the One. Being one with *being* is living consciously, finding the gift in the moment. Try setting aside time to be with yourself. Time in the silence nourishes your spirit.

Doing What You Love

Once you are clear on how you are spending your time – *doing* things mindlessly or *being* present in the moment – the question becomes *what are you doing*? Are you spending your time on life-affirming activities that make you happy and move you toward your goals? Are you working on your priorities? Are you taking time to create balance and fun in your life? Are you nurturing your mind, body, and spirit?

Finding the Joy

Take responsibility for your *soaring* attitude and increase your *soaring* altitude. Identify what creates joy in your life and then do it. What does that look like for you? For example, if you set aside a specific time for family and friends in your schedule, you are more likely to spend time with them.

Family and friends are sources of support and nurturance, and those feelings work both ways: We nurture and we are nourished. Building and maintaining a social support system of individuals who love and nurture you are important to your overall sense of well-being.

Take a look at the eight areas of the **Soaring Life Balance Scale** on the next page (Figure 3). Change or add categories on the chart to fit your own life. Rate the level of satisfaction you currently feel in each area of your life by placing a dot on the chart in that area. Draw a line to create a graph of your level of satisfaction with your current life balance.

Next, using a different-colored pen, rate how you would like to spend your time in each area of your life. Draw a dotted line to connect the dots. The difference between the two lines represents opportunity for you to create more balance in your life. Using this information, what goals would you like to set? Create time to do what you love to nurture your spirit and bring more balance in your life.

The *Soaring* Life Balance Scale

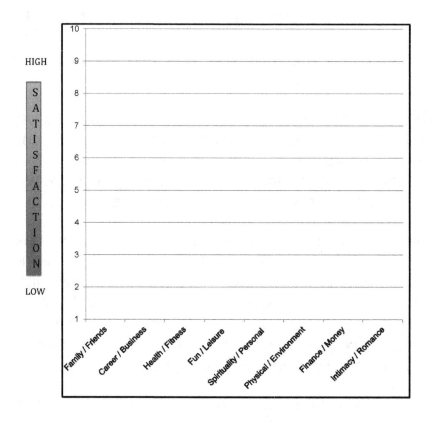

Figure 3

Lightening Up

Taking a light approach to living and looking on the brighter side of life are ongoing approaches to nurture the soul. Look for the light in the situation. Bringing levity into a situation can remove the sting and help us feel better. Feelings, thoughts, and attitudes play major roles in our overall sense of well-being. Humor allows us to step back and disconnect from fear and anxiety around an event. It provides an opportunity to see things from a different perspective. Humor keeps us balanced. Use humor to lighten your mental and emotional outlook to help you during loss and pain. Using humor during times of stress can lift our spirits and facilitate *soaring*.

We can de-stress by taking the high road and looking on the positive side of situations. There is always a lighter side in any situation. If you worry about money, you can list all the wonderful things you are grateful for – your home, your car, and your other assets.

What is there to appreciate? What can you be grateful for? The glass is always half full.

Create happiness! Laugh until you cry! Laughter massages your internal organs, stimulates the flow of positive endorphins, and lightens up your demeanor. And let's not forget the power of love.

Expressing Love

Be love in action. Express love wherever you go – on the subway, on the freeway, in the elevator. Activate love and compassion in your experiences and love will create a kinder, gentler you. Your life will change. You will transform. Become a poster person for love and allow the Law of Attraction and the Law of Giving and Receiving to attract loving relationships into your life.

What does love have to do with living a purpose-filled life? Love has *everything* to do with a life of connection and fulfillment! If you don't know where to start, begin with a smile, a nod of recognition, a simple hello to people you meet, and see where the road leads.

Nurturing the spirit is finding inner peace and harmony. It is recognizing the Divine Presence within and connecting with Presence through prayer and meditation. It is grounding ourselves in love. Nurturing oneness with Spirit and with each other awakens our inner spirits through love, joy, and connection with family and friends.

Although discussed separately, remember that all body systems are intricately related. Nurturing any part of the mind/body/spirit system nurtures the other. Continuing these *soaring* practices on a regular basis moves you consistently up to *soaring* altitude.

Applying This *Flight Lesson* in Your Life

1. What activities nurture your spirit?

2. Plan a minimum of one activity a week to nurture your mind, body, or spirit. For example, get a massage, go to a movie, visit a museum, see a play, get a manicure or pedicure, go to a ball game, or watch sports on TV.

3. Schedule social time with family and friends.

4. Spend time daily in prayer, meditation, and contemplation.

5. Make an Action Plan. What action steps can you take to balance your life?

My Life Balance Action Plan

Goal:

What	How	Who	When
1.			
2.			
3.			
4.			
5.			

Goal:

What	How	Who	When
1.			
2.			
3.			
4.			
5.			

FLIGHT LESSON TWELVE

Soaring:
Living Empowered and Joyful

Aware of my spiritual essence, I recognize that there is something going on in my life that I cannot see. There is an Invisible Presence always with me, the evidence and footprints of which are clear. This is Intelligence, the Power for Good in the Universe that I access for inspiration and guidance. Through this Intelligence I co-create my world. I feel empowered and joyful, confident that the power of the Universe is supporting me. When we began this flight together, I posited that you, too, can live a life of joy and power by recognizing the power within you. Through Spirit we access this power.

I am clear on my purpose. I have a plan for this phase of my journey, knowing that my passion inspires and calls me. I live in joy and gratitude. I love and appreciate life. My aim is to be kind and compassionate and help others.

Daily I court the Presence in prayer and meditation. Often my prayer is a simple "Thank you." Since my thoughts are prayers I realize that I am always praying. When requested, I also pray for others and hold the light for their visions. I spend time in the silence during which I experience inner peace and regeneration. When in the silence, I ask for guidance and receive direction. What a joy-filled life I am living today!

I am in harmony with the Universe, and in the flow of life. I realize that *"There is a time for everything and a season for every activity under the heavens"* (Ecclesiastes 3:1). When it is my time to learn from an experience, I look for the lesson to be learned, find the peace, forgive, and move on.

Although some experiences may hurt or wound me, I realize that this, too, is a part of this wonderful experience called life. I realize that every new beginning has an ending. I look for the magic. I look for the gift and stay with the pain and hurt for as long as it takes to heal, say good-bye to the experience, and make a new beginning.

Maintaining *soaring altitude* is a continuing goal as I look to Spirit to maintain life balance daily, *doing* what I love, while remembering to focus on *being* and release childhood tapes to *get it done quickly and correctly.*

I nurture my body with daily walks, strength-training twice a week, and yoga classes. I am primarily a vegetarian, moving in and out of veganism as circumstances allow. Supported by a loving family and community, I enjoy life. Periodically I go to my health retreat for quiet time and detoxification.

Life is great. I have learned to *soar* over the currents. When it is my time to lead, I do so with love. When it is my time to fall into formation, I do so with grace and ease.

I mindfully *soar* through life, realizing that there are different levels of *soaring*. I can *soar* like an eagle with power and thrust, or I can *soar* gracefully like a sea gull. My soul's assignment is to burn the brightest flame of love and light and facilitate others in shining their lights. Each day I *soar* in love, and in Spirit I achieve that aim.

Putting It All Together

Now is your opportunity to integrate all the *Soaring Flight Lessons* into your life. You do so easily and comfortably. You are living your best life unencumbered and joyful.

With inner peace and calm you are now *soaring*, flying on autopilot. You have practiced and internalized your *Flight Lessons*. You now have an active spiritual practice that inspires and supports you. The Universe continues to call you, push you forward, and express through your visions, dreams, hopes, and expectations. At *soaring* altitude, you feel your oneness, your wholeness with the Divine and all of life. Your dreams, visions, and purpose propel you forward. You are inspired. Faith is the wind beneath your wings. You are love in action. You greet others on the path with you with "*Namaste*," which means "The God in me recognizes the God in you." You love and appreciate yourself as well as others *soaring* with you. Expressing love and kindness to others enriches your life as well as the lives of others.

Our purpose here is to learn, grow, and unfold; to live a life of meaning and purpose based on our own hopes, desires, and aspirations. Just as the acorn's destiny is to be an oak tree, your destiny is to discover and live in alignment with the power within you; to live life empowered and joyful. You are now clear on your purpose. You are living your vision day to day, knowing that as you grow and change your vision expands and changes. You are always becoming more – more love, more joy to yourself and others. Your vision draws you, inspires you, and beckons you upward. You know where you want to go and what has meaning for you. At any point that you want to change direction, you envision your next step.

You are living your dream daily, in mind, in consciousness, and in action as you mindfully go about the business of life. In your mind's eye you see and feel your goal accomplished. You use creative visualization to live from your dream as you take appropriate action.

> Outlaw and his wife, Kandy, are *soaring*. They are loving, sincere, purpose-driven people. Outlaw's purpose is "to deliberately and intentionally" make a difference every day. His goal is to make a difference in at least three people's lives daily. He accomplishes this by "engaging, energizing, and empowering" people to understand their purpose and create win-win situations in all aspects of their lives – employment, family, and personal development.

Spirituality is central to their lives. Outlaw begins his day connecting with the "Omnipotent" in prayer and meditation, and prays multiple times a day, both silently and out loud. He then meditates for an hour aimed toward perfect stillness in which to plant the seeds of his vision into his consciousness. After reaching a point of stillness and connection, he then participates in what he refers to as the "I AM Mirror Exercise" for mental conditioning, believing strongly that anything that follows *I AM* ("I AM THAT I AM" – Exodus 3:14) shapes his reality. He looks into his eyes and affirms his vision and purpose, or anything that he wants to show up in his life. This has been his practice for thirty years. When he was a child his mother instilled in him the belief that to achieve you must believe you are one of the chosen few. He uses the mirror practice to imbed any belief that he wants in his life into his consciousness.

Spirituality is also central to Kandy's life. She, too, prays daily and practices mindfulness meditation in the energy of their garden. Kandy believes in Divine order and perceives a connection with the Infinite in which she hears God's plan for her life through conscious awareness and actively listening to spiritual messages at church, in Biblical readings, and in daily living. Faith and gratitude are major components of their spiritual practices.

Kandy's reaction to turbulence is to feel the pain and then take appropriate action to move through it. Outlaw does not view turbulence as an issue in his life. He looks at issues in two ways: those he can control and those he cannot. He surrenders to issues he cannot control and looks to problem-solving to resolve others.

Outlaw practices self-care by being conscious of his diet, working out daily, surrounding himself with like-minded people, and reaching out to people he loves. Love is the "combustion" that makes their lives and family unit run. The family lives by core values: love, support, education, excellence, respect, and honesty in their relationships and spirituality.

Kandy and Outlaw *soar* like eagles, strong and powerful, aware of their Source. They are intentionally making a difference through love, compassion, faith, and selfless service while they pursue their passion as performance consultants.

Soaring is reaching a point in consciousness where you let go of fear and doubt. It is reaching the realization that there is a Power for Good in the Universe, and that when you live in harmony with the Power for Good and your faith, it empowers you. You co-create your experiences based on your own desires. Although life changes and crises occur, your innate connection to Spirit supports and sustains you in navigating turbulence.

Loretta, a retired spiritual leader and prolific author of over eighty books, recently experienced a health challenge. After a lengthy period of rehabilitation of the lumbar spine, she has returned to writing her spiritual blog and is seeking to get her creative juices flowing. She is working on two new books as well as teaching a class. Her physicians are amazed at her progress. She lives in gratitude, has a daily spiritual practice, and a prayer partner. She *soars* in mind and spirit as she continues to make a loving contribution to the world, confident of her ability to experience a full recovery.

Loretta *soars* like a sea gull, full of grace and ease, empowered by her wisdom, a strong belief in a Power for Good in the Universe, and prayer. She is full of love and optimism as she shares her light with the world through her books, classes, and spiritual counseling.

As you *soar*, you are aware of your connection to Spirit and the Divine within you. You are in control of your life because you know that your thoughts create your experiences.

Knowing that you are always thinking into the creative realm, you think about what you want in your life, not what you do not want. You let go of fear and have faith in God and in yourself. When doubt arises, you use your faith and positive affirmations to work through the fear. Even though obstacles occur, you have *soaring* practices to address them: prayer, meditation, optimism, and belief that the goodness of life will sustain you. As issues arise in your life, you take them to the altar of your higher self and go within. In the silence you pray and practice the Presence in whatever way best suits you. You live in gratitude and appreciation. Gratitude attracts more abundance to you.

You consciously seek to spend time with friends and family to build a support system around you, seeking support from loved ones and professionals as needed. Life is not perfect, yet life is good. An attitude of joy, optimism, and gratitude make it so. Although some days test your optimism, you continue to trust and believe.

You use creative visualization to live your dream, creating visual images such as vision boards or treasure maps as reminders. In your mind's eye you see and feel the life you are seeking. Periodically you check in with your purpose. You live in alignment with your purpose, modifying and changing it as needed. As you change and grow, so does your vision and world-view. Life is not automatic; it is smoother, empowered by your spiritual connection. You co-create your experiences.

When things occur to hurt your feelings or wound your spirit, you use the opportunities to practice forgiveness. Taking time to acknowledge the pain, you move from the victim's role and put your energy to work in support of your dreams. Feeling a sense of power, you ask yourself, "What was the gift of the experience? What did I learn from the experience to propel me upward?" Answering these questions, you feel an even greater sense of power.

You schedule time to pamper yourself and nurture your spirit, resting as needed. Just as you put in a full day of other purposeful activity, you take time to regenerate your spirit. Perhaps you have a massage, an evening at the theater, a movie, a round of golf, a day at the races, lunch with friends. You choose.

You consciously do things to brighten your day as well as that of others. Random acts of kindness make you feel good. Thank-you notes lift the spirits of others, and in writing them they lift yours. In the giving you receive.

You spend time in nature to connect with life and brighten your day. You aim toward reducing the busyness of your day that I refer to as doing and spend more time being – *being in love and service.* You take time to listen to your heart's song. Letting go of the voices in your head, you tune in to your Divine Essence and you *soar*!

When you encounter turbulence, you return to your center and rely on your faith and Divine guidance. You are aware that the Divine Essence within you points the way forward. You go within and listen to your intuition – that still, inner voice. Practicing your faith, you rely on prayer and meditation. In the stillness you ask your higher self for direction and guidance, knowing the answer is within.

Practices that bring you into the present also move your spirit into the Presence. They give you a new lease on life. They energize you and you *soar.* More than that, life takes on a new meaning. They help you realize that the change you are seeking is occurring.

You are *soaring*, living empowered and joyful.

Applying This *Flight Lesson* in Your Life

1. Maintaining *soaring* altitude requires ongoing practice. Review the *Soaring* Action Chart, (Figure 4) to help integrate the *Flight Less*ons into your daily life and keep your flight airborne.

2. Use the *Soaring* Master Calendar (Figure 5) to schedule the activities you choose into the calendar.

3. Envision your dream and visualize it daily in your mind until you see it in your life.

4. Pray on a daily basis to connect to Spirit, the source of your power.

5. Connect with your breath on a daily basis as a source of peace and guidance.

6. Love yourself and others as sources of joy, happiness, and fulfillment.

7. Practice mindfulness. Appreciate life by being fully aware of what is going on in the moment.

8. Practice the "I AM Mirror Exercise" daily. Look into your eyes and say, "I AM," and follow it with a statement of your dream, what you want to see in your life.

9. Live and express gratitude.

10. Schedule personal nurturing activities to take care of your mind, body, and spirit.

11. Review and modify your *Flight Plan* as needed.

12. Select and apply the appropriate *Flight Lesson* when encountering turbulence.

Happy *soaring*! Enjoy living empowered and joyful!

The *Soaring* Action Chart

Flight Lesson	Soaring Practice	Impact
The *Soaring* Flight Plan	Expand your world view. Open to new ways of doing and being.	Live a life of personal power and joy.
Awakening Your Spirituality	Recognize one Universal Power. Believe the Power is within you. Think positive thoughts.	Positive thoughts garner positive results. Control the circumstances in your life.
Developing Your Flight Plan	Clarify your purpose and vision. Dream Big. Review and modify your plan.	Clarification of purpose helps you get what you want from life and positions you to *soar*.
Visualize It! Picture It! Affirm It!	Visualize your desired outcomes. Make a collage. Affirm your desires.	Co-creates your experiences. Achieves the results you desire.
Igniting Love	Love yourself. Express unconditional love. Become love.	Love lifts the spirit, provides feelings of well-being and happiness, and increases altitude.
Lifting Off with Gratitude	Express gratitude to Spirit and all that enriches your life. Express random acts of kindness.	Raises energy vibrations for yourself and others, enabling you to *soar* with an attitude of gratitude.
Praying to Increase Altitude	Develop a daily prayer practice to realize your Higher Power and connect with your higher self.	Changes conditions and circumstances in your life. Increases optimism.

Figure 4

Flight Lesson	Soaring Practice	Impact
Meditating to Regenerate Your Spirit	Meditate daily. Explore and select a meditation practice to fit your lifestyle.	Experiencing your Higher Power accesses inner wisdom, increases relaxation, reduces stress.
Forgiving to Forget	Forgive others and take back your power.	Frees energy to work on your priorities. Regains power.
Encountering Turbulence	Use a variety of *soaring* practices such as positive thinking, prayer, and faith, as needed.	Empowers you to remain calm and resolve life crises with confidence.
Nurturing Mind, Body, and Spirit	Engage in self-care activities to lift your spirits and build your support system.	A healthier, happier lifestyle.
Soaring: Living Empowered and Joyful	Incorporate the *soaring* practices in your lifestyle and practice as needed.	A happy, joy-filled, spiritual, empowered lifestyle

Figure 4
(continued)

The *Soaring* Master Calendar

To create your *soaring* lifestyle, schedule your *soaring* practices such as exercise, meditation, and prayer into the ***Soaring* Master Calendar**.

Sun	Mon	Tue	Wed	Thur	Fri	Sat

Figure 5

Printed in the United States
By Bookmasters